W9-BMG-984

More Piggyback Songs

New Songs Sung to the Tunes of Childhood Favorites

Totline Press
Warren Publishing House
P.O. Box 2255, Everett, WA 98203

More Piggyback Songs

compiled from songs
contributed to the
Totline
Newsletter

Illustrated by Marion Hopping Ekberg

Chorded by Barbara Robinson

ACKNOWLEDGEMENTS

I wish to thank all the "TOTLINE" subscribers who have enthusiasticly contributed more "Piggyback Songs" for this second book.

I wish to thank Barbara Robinson for again chording all our songs.

And a very special thanks to Marion Ekberg for her delightful drawings.

Jean Warren

Copyright © 1984 Jean Warren

All rights reserved, except for the inclusion of brief quotations in a review, no part of this book may be reproduced in any form without the written permission of the publisher.

ISBN   0-911019-02-2

Library of Congress Catalogue Card Number 84-90020
Illustrated by Marion Hopping Ekberg
Cover Design by Larry Countryman
Chorded by Barbara Robinson
Manufactured in the United States of America
Published by Warren Publishing House, P.O. Box 2255, Everett, WA 98203

Distributed by:

GRYPHON HOUSE, INC.
P.O. Box 275
Mt. Rainier, MD 20712

CONTENTS

Songs About Winter

Songs About Spring

CONTENTS

Songs About Summer

Songs About Fall

CONTENTS

Songs About School

CONTENTS

Songs About Me

Songs About Animals

Songs Just For Fun

SONGS ABOUT WINTER

SNOWMAN, SNOWMAN

Sung to: "Twinkle, Twinkle Little Star"

```
C            C         F          C
Snowman, snowman, where did you go?

   G7          C       G7        C
I built you yesterday out of snow.

     C         G7        C        G7
I built you high and I built you fat.

   C         G7       C         G7
I put on eyes and nose and a hat.

        C                        F      C
And now you're gone - all melted away.

         G7        C      G7         C
But it's sunny outside, so I'll go and play.
```

Carole Sick
Hershey, PA

CHRISTMAS TIME IS HERE

Sung to: "Mary Had a Little Lamb"

F   F
Five little reindeer prancing up and down

  C   F
prancing up and down, prancing up and down

F   F
Five little reindeer prancing up and down

         C   F
For Christmas time is here.

(Children prance in place, bending elbows in front of them with hands bent down like hoofs)

F   F
Four little Santa elves trimming up the tree

  C   F
trimming up the tree, trimming up the tree

F   F
Four little Santa elves trimming up the tree

         C   F
For Christmas time is here.

(Children pretend to trim an imaginary tree)

This song can be used as a finger play or action poem. It can also be used as a simple Christmas program using props and/or costumes.

Everyone sings the song while selected children stand up for special parts.

PROPS NEEDED:

Five   Reindeer Headbands
        Use brown construction paper - fold in half to cut out antlers. Add additional strip for headband.

Four   Christmas Ornaments
        Make ornaments out of cardboard. Make triangle trees or circle balls. Color the glue and then have an assortment of material (such as: rick-rack and glitter) to make collages. Punch hole at the top and make a yarn hanger.

Three Sets of Jingle Bells
        Put 3 or 4 bells on yarn or leather.

Two   Snowflakes
        Fold square of white paper and cut out designs.

One   Star
        Cut a paper plate into a 5-pointed star. Paint yellow and add glitter around the edges.

Barbara Fletcher
El Cajon, CA

F   F
Three little jingle bells ringing in the night

  C   F
ringing in the night, ringing in the night

F   F
Three little jingle bells ringing in the night

         C   F
For Christmas time is here.

(Children shake one hand pretending to ring bells)

F   F
Two little snowflakes twirling round and round

  C   F
twirling round and round, twirling round and round

C   F
Two little snowflakes twirling round and round

         C   F
For Christmas time is here.

(Children twirl in place)

F   F
One little twinkling star shining big and bright

  C   F
big and bright, big and bright

F   F
One little twinkling star shining big and bright

         C   F
For Christmas time is here.

(Child stands with arms outstretched)

CHRISTMAS TIME IS NEAR

Sung to: "Farmer in the Dell"

F
Christmas time is near.

F
Christmas time is near.

F
Merry Christmas everyone.

F   C   F
Christmas time is near.

F
It's time to trim the tree.

F
It's time to trim the tree.

F
Merry Christmas everyone.

     F   C   F
It's time to trim the tree.

F
It's time to wrap the gifts.

F
It's time to wrap the gifts.

F
Merry Christmas everyone.

     F   C   F
It's time to wrap the gifts.

F
It's time to hang the stocking.

F
It's time to hang the stocking.

F
Merry Christmas everyone.

     F   C   F
It's time to hang the stocking.

F
Santa will soon be here.

F
Santa will soon be here.

F
Merry Christmas everyone.

F   C   F
Santa will soon be here.

Betty Ruth Baker
Waco, TX

CHRISTMAS TIME

Sung to: "Farmer in the Dell"

F
Christmas Time is here

F
Christmas Time is here

F
Hustle Bustle Busy Time

     F   C7   F
As Christmas Time is here.

F
Christmas Trees are up

F
Christmas Trees are up

F
Tinsel balls and Popcorn too

     F   C7   F
As Christmas Time is here.

F
Santa Claus is here

F
Santa Claus is here

F
Bringing Gifts and Stockings too

     F   C7   F
As Christmas Time is here.

Kristine Wagoner
Pacific, WA

CHRISTMAS GAME

Sung to: "Mary Had A Little Lamb"

C   C
Christmas time will soon be here,

G7   C
Soon be here, soon be here.

C   C
Christmas time will soon be here,

G7   C
Happiest time of all the year.

C   C
Clap your hands with Christmas cheer,

G7   C
Christmas cheer, Christmas cheer.

C   C
Clap your hands with Christmas cheer,

G7   C
Happiest time of all the year.

C   C
Skip around with Christmas cheer,

G7   C
Christmas cheer, Christmas cheer.

C   C
Skip around with Christmas cheer,

G7   C
Happiest time of all the year.

C   C
Walk around with Christmas cheer,

G7   C
Christmas cheer, Christmas cheer.

C   C
Walk around with Christmas cheer,

G7   C
Happiest time of all the year.

C   C
Tiptoe around with Christmas cheer,

G7   C
Christmas cheer, Christmas cheer.

C   C
Tiptoe around with Christmas cheer,

G7   C
Happiest time of all the year.

C   C
Hop around with Christmas cheer,

G7   C
Christmas cheer, Christmas cheer.

C   C
Hop around with Christmas cheer.

G7   C
Happiest time of all the year.

C   C
Wave to your friends with Christmas cheer,

G7   C
Christmas cheer, Christmas cheer.

C   C
Wave to your friends with Christmas cheer,

G7   C
Happiest time of all the year.

C   C
Dance around with Christmas cheer,

G7   C
Christmas cheer, Christmas cheer.

C   C
Dance around with Christmas cheer,

G7   C
Happiest time of all the year.

(Children form circle, holding hands and sing the first verse. Then in the circle do movement with each verse. Encourage the children to be creative with the last verse with choice of movement. Exercise such as touch your toes, bend your knees, stretch your arms, could be substituted for the movement.)

Betty Ruth Baker
Waco, TX

THE MERRY CHRISTMAS BAND

Sung to: "Mary Had a Little Lamb"

C   C
Play the band, it's Christmas time,

G   C
Christmas time, Christmas time.

C   C
Play the band, it's Christmas time.

G   C
Merry Christmas time.

C   C
Ring the bells, it's Christmas time,

G   C
Christmas time, Christmas time.

C   C
Ring the bells, it's Christmas time.

G   C
Merry Christmas time.

C   C
Tap the sticks, it's Christmas time,

G   C
Christmas time, Christmas time.

C   C
Tap the sticks, it's Christmas time.

G   C
Merry Christmas time.

C   C
Play the tambourines, it's Christmas time,

G   C
Christmas time, Christmas time.

C   C
Play the tambourines, it's Christmas time.

G   C
Merry Christmas time.

C   C
Clang the cymbals, it's Christmas time,

G   C
Christmas time, Christmas time.

C   C
Clang the cymbals, it's Christmas time.

G   C
Merry Christmas time.

C   C
Beat the drum, it's Christmas time,

G   C
Christmas time, Christmas time.

C   C
Beat the drum, it's Christmas time.

G   C
Merry Christmas time.

C   C
Play the triangle, it's Christmas time,

G   C
Christmas time, Christmas time.

C   C
Play the triangle, it's Christmas time.

G   C
Merry Christmas time.

C   C
Play the band, it's Christmas time,

G   C
Christmas time, Christmas time.

C   C
Play the band, it's Christmas time.

G   C
Merry Christmas time.

Materials Needed: Rhythm Instruments.

Betty Ruth Baker
Waco, TX

S - A - N - T - A

Sung to: "BINGO"

I know a man with a long white beard
F   Bb   F

And Santa is his name-o
    F   C   F

S - A - N - T - A
F   Bb

S - A - N - T - A
C   F

S - A - N - T - A
Dm   Gm

And Santa is his name-o.
    C7   F

He slides down the chimney with a pack on his back
        F   Bb   F

And Santa is his name-o
    F   C   F

S - A - N - T - A
F   Bb

S - A - N - T - A
C   F

S - A - N - T - A
Dm   Gm

And Santa is his name-o.
    C7   F

Eight little reindeer pull his sleigh
F   Bb   F

And Santa is his name-o
    F   C   F

S - A - N - T - A
F   Bb

S - A - N - T - A
C   F

S - A - N - T - A
Dm   Gm

And Santa is his name-o.
    C7   F

Linda Robinson
Centerville, MA

SANTA'S COMING

Sung to: "Frere Jacques"

F
Santa's coming,

F
Santa's coming,

F
Sleigh bells ring,

F
Sleigh bells ring,

F
It is Christmas Eve,

F
It is Christmas Eve.

F
Ding, Ding, Dong.

F
Ding, Ding, Dong.

Kathryn Brickey
Huntington Beach, CA

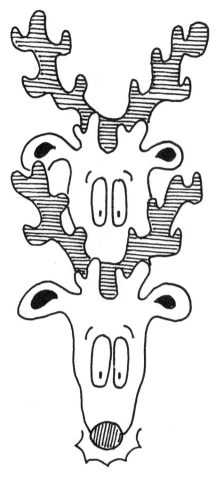

HE'LL BE DRIVING EIGHT BROWN REINDEER

Sung to: "She'll Be Coming Round The Mountain"

                      F
Oh, he'll be driving eight brown reindeer when he comes.

         F   C
He'll be driving eight brown reindeer when he comes.

         F
He'll be driving eight brown reindeer,

         Bb
He'll be driving eight brown reindeer,

         F   C   F
He'll be driving eight brown reindeer when he comes.

                   F
Oh, he'll be piled up with toys when he comes

         F   C
He'll be piled up with toys when he comes

         F
He'll be piled up with toys,

         Bb
For the good girls and boys.

         F   C   F
He'll be piled up with toys when he comes.

               F
Oh, he'll be dressed all in red when he comes

         F
He'll be dressed all in red when he comes

         F
He'll be dressed all in red,

         Bb
From his toes up to his head.

         F   C   F
He'll be dressed all in red when he comes.

Jean Warren

RUDOLPH'S LIGHT

Sung to: "Camptown Races"

C
Reindeers pull on Santa's sleigh

G7   G7
Ho-Ho*   Ho-Ho*

C
Rudolph's leading all the way

G7   C
Ho-Ho-Ho-Ho-Ho*

C
Gonna ride all day

F   C
Gonna ride all night

C
He'll be riding through the sky

G7   C
Using Rudolph's light!
******

(*Ring bells at this point)

Judy Hall
Wytheville, VA

CHRISTMAS COOKIES

Sung to: "Frere Jacques"

C
Christmas cookies,

C
Christmas cookies,

C
Mom just made,

C
Mom just made,

   C
A star, a bell, a tree.

C
Which should I save?

    C
I'll eat all three,

C
Yum, yum, eee.

Saundra Winnett
Fort Worth, TX

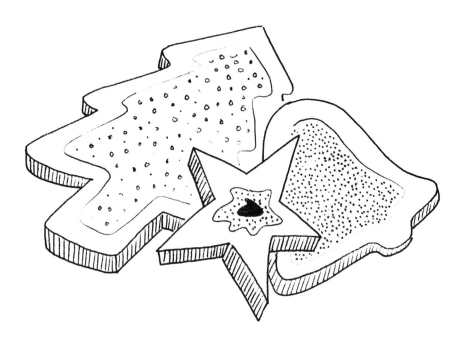

MERRY CHRISTMAS EVERYWHERE

Sung to: "Old MacDonald Had a Farm"

 F   Bb   F
Christmas time will soon be here.

 F   C7   F
Merry Christmas time.

 F   Bb   F
Happiest time of all the year.

 F   C7   F
Merry Christmas time.

 F
Merry Christmas here.

 F
Merry Christmas there

 F
Christmas cheer is everywhere.

 F   Bb   F
Christmas time will soon be here.

 F   C   F
Merry Christmas time.

Betty Ruth Baker
Waco, TX

SMELLS LIKE CHRISTMAS

Sung to: "Frere Jacques"

F   F
Smells like Christmas, smells like Christmas

F   F
Mmmm so good, mmmm so good

F   F
I can smell the pine tree, I can smell the cookies

F   F
Mmmm so good, mmmm so good.

Jean Warren

GINGERBREAD BOY

Sung to: "The Muffin Man"

      F   F
Oh, will you bake a gingerbread boy,

    G7
   A gingerbread boy,

    C7
   A gingerbread boy,

   A gingerbread boy,

 F
Oh, will you bake a gingerbread boy

  G7   C   F
Then put him in the oven.

      F   F
Oh, will you eat the gingerbread boy

     G7
The gingerbread boy,

     C7
The gingerbread boy,

The gingerbread boy,

    F
Oh, will you eat the gingerbread boy

     G7   C   F
Then take him out right now.

Joyce Marshall
Whitby, Ontario
Canada

GINGERBREAD

Sung to: "Frere Jacques"

C   C
Gingerbread, Gingerbread,

C
Yum, yum, yum,

C
Yum, yum, yum.

C   C
I like gingerbread, I like gingerbread,

C
In my tum,

C
In my tum.

Joyce Marshall
Whitby, Ontario
Canada

19

I'M A CHRISTMAS TREE

Sung to: "I'm A Little Teapot"

C   F   C
I'm a great big Christmas tree, tall and straight.

F   C   G7   C
Here are my branches for you to decorate.

C   C   F   C
First we'll put the star up on the top,

F   C   G7   C
But be careful that the ornaments don't drop.

Linda Robinson
Centerville, MA

LITTLE GREEN TREE

Sung to: "I'm a Little Teapot"

C   C
I'm a little green tree

       F   C
       Short and sparse,

F   C
Here is my trunk

       G7   C
       And here is my bough.

C   C
Decorate me all up

       F   C
       With bright lights,

F   C
Then plug me in and

       G7   C
       Watch me shine!

Billie Taylor
Sioux City, IA

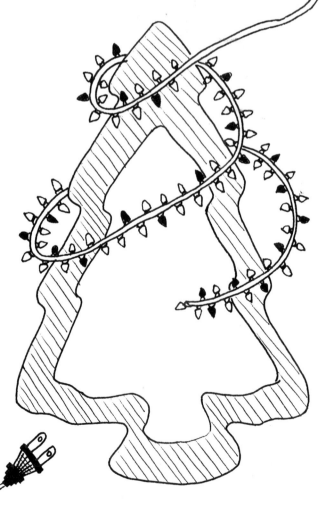

20

SNOWFLAKES

Sung to: "Grey Squirrel"

C   G   C
Snowflakes, snowflakes, falling on the ground
C   G   C
Snowflakes, snowflakes, falling all around.

C
I am bundled to my chin.

C
See my footprints where I've been.

C   G   C
Snowflakes, snowflakes, falling on the ground.

Frank Dally
Akeny, IA

IT IS SNOWING

Sung to: "Frere Jacques"

C   C
It is snowing, it is snowing
C   C
All around, all around
C
Soft and quiet snowflakes
C
Soft and quiet snowflakes
C   C
Not a sound, not a sound.

Saundra Winnett
Fort Worth, TX

BUILD A SNOWMAN

Sung to: "Frere Jacques"

C   C
Build a snowman, build a snowman
C   C
Big and round, big and round,
C
Sun is shining on him
C
Sun is shining on him
C   C
He's all gone, he's all gone.

Saundra Winnett
Fort Worth, TX

SNOWFLAKES FALLING DOWN

Sung to: "Row, Row, Row Your Boat"

C   C
Snowflakes falling down,
     (Wiggle fingers downward)
C   C
Falling on the ground.
C   C
Great, big white flakes
     (Make circles with thumbs and forefingers touching)
G   C
That do not make a sound.
     (Finger to lips and shake head "no")

Susan A. Miller
Kutztown, PA

ON GROUNDHOG'S DAY

Sung to: "Mary Had a Little Lamb"

C   C
Do you see your shadow,

    G   C
   shadow, shadow?

C   C
Do you see your shadow?

G   C
On Groundhog's Day.

C   C
Yes, I see my shadow,

    G   C
   shadow, shadow,

C   C
Yes, I see my shadow

G   C
On Groundhog's Day.

C   C
I don't see my shadow,

    G   C
   shadow, shadow

C   C
I don't see my shadow

G   C
On Groundhog's Day.

Betty Ruth Baker
Waco, TX

LITTLE GROUNDHOG

Sung to: "Frere Jacques"

C
Little Groundhog

C
Little Shadow

C
Where are you?

C
Where are you?

C
Groundhog's Day is here

C
Spring will be here too

C
Wake up you

C
Wake up you.

Kristine Wagoner
Pacific, WA

MR. GROUNDHOG

Sung to: "Frere Jacques"

C   C
Mr. Groundhog, Mr. Groundhog,

C   C
Are you there? Are you there?

C
Will you see your shadow,

C
We all want to know,

C   C
Groundhog Day, Groundhog Day.

Dr. Margery A. Kranyik
Hyde Park, MA

SEE MY SHADOW

Sung to: "Frere Jacques"

C   C
See my shadow, see my shadow,

C   C
Move this way, move this way,

C   C
Doing things that I do, doing things that I do,

C   C
Follow me, follow me.

Saundra Winnett
Fort Worth, TX

VALENTINES RED

Sung to: "Lavender's Blue"

C   C7
Valentines red, dilly, dilly

F   C
Valentines blue,

C
Valentines all pink and frilly,

D7   G7
Say "I love you!"

C   C7
Flowers and lace, dilly, dilly,

F   C
Pretty cards, too,

C
Valentines covered with hearts,

D7   G7   C
Say "I love you."

Eleanor G. Thomas
Princeton, NJ

MY VALENTINE

Sung to: "The Muffin Man"

     F   F
It's nice to have a friend like you.

   G7   C
I'll tell you what I'm going to do.

    F   F
Because you make me feel so fine,

  G7   C   F
I'll take you for my Valentine.

Frank Dally
Akeny, IA

PUSSY IN THE TREE

Sung to: "Mary Had a Little Lamb"

C   C
Pussy, pussy high in the tree

      G   C
high in the tree, high in the tree

C   C
Pussy, pussy high in the tree

      G   C
Won't you come and play with me?

C   C
Pussy, pussy soft as a pillow

      G   C
soft as a pillow, soft as a pillow

C   C
Pussy, pussy soft as a pillow

G   C
You're my little pussy willow.

Jean Warren

23

GEORGE WASHINGTON

Sung to: "Yankee Doodle"

    C   C   G7
One time there was a little boy

    C   G
Who had a little hatchet.

    C   F
He looked and looked around to find

 G7   C
A little tree to catch it.

     C   C   G7
At last he spied a cherry tree

    C   G
His father's pride and joy.

    C   F
He chopped it down, right to the ground.

   G7   C
My! What a naughty boy!

     C   C   G7
And then he heard an angry voice.

    C   G
It sounded like a cymbal.

        C   F
George knew he was in trouble great.

   G7   C
And he began to tremble.

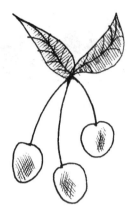

     C   C   G7
Who cut this tree, my son did you?

   C   G
His father asked the question.

    C   F
Yes, it was I. I can not lie.

 G7   C
I cut it with my hatchet!

CHORUS:

F   F   C
Georgie, Georgie, no, no, no,

       C   C
Be careful what you do.

         F   F
Hatchets can be dangerous

     C C   C
And you might get hurt, too!

Betty Ruth Baker
Waco, TX

WHO WAS THOMAS EDISON?

Sung to: "Mary Had a Little Lamb"

C   C   G   C
Who was Thomas Edison, Edison, Edison?

C   G   C
He invented something nice we use every night.

C   C   G   C
Can you guess what it is, what it is, what it is,

C   C   G   C
Can you guess what it is, we use every night?

(Electric light)

Saundra Winnett
Fort Worth, TX

24

SONGS ABOUT SPRING

SPRINGTIME

Sung to: "Skip to My Lou"

C   C
Springtime, Springtime, how do you do?

G7   G7
Springtime, Springtime, how do you do?

C   C
Springtime, Springtime, glad to see you.

G7   C
Flowers, sunshine are part of you.

C   C
Springtime colors everywhere,

G7   G7
Springtime colors everywhere,

C   C
Bright and cheerful colors too

G7   C
Blossoms, buds and greenery too.

C   C
Springtime animals everywhere,

G7   G7
Springtime animals everywhere,

C   C
Birds, bees and butterflies too

G7   C   C
Springtime, Springtime glad to see you.

Kristine Wagoner
Pacific, WA

IT IS SPRINGTIME

Sung to: "London Bridge"

C
Leaves are growing on the trees,

      G   C
on the trees, on the trees,

C
Leaves are growing on the trees,

G   C
It is springtime.

Other Verses:

C   C
All the grass is turning green . . .

C   C
See the birdies build their nest . . .

C   C
Watch the flowers start to grow . . .

Frank Dally
Ankeny, IA

WHEN I LOOK INTO THE SKY

Sung to: "Twinkle, Twinkle Little Star"

   C   C   F   C
When I look into the sky

G7   C   G7   C
I can see the clouds go by.

C   G7 C   G7
They don't ever make a sound.

 C   G7   C   G7
Letting wind push them around.

C   C   F   C
Some go fast and some go slow.

  G7   C   G7   C
I wonder where the clouds all go.

Frank Dally
Ankeny, IA

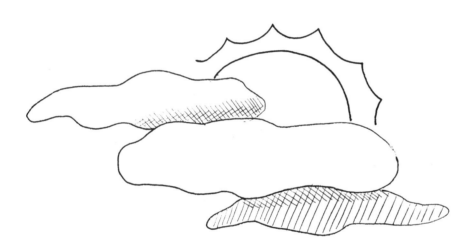

I SEE THE WIND

Sung to: "Here We Go Around
the Mulberry Bush"

       F
I see the wind

When the leaves dance by

 C7
I see the wind

When the clothes wave "Hi!"

     F
I see the wind

When the trees bend low

  C7
I see the wind

         F
When the flags all blow.

     F
I see the wind

When the kites fly high

  C7
I see the wind

When the clouds float by

  F
I see the wind

When it blows my hair

  C7
I see the wind

    F
Most everywhere.

Jean Warren

26

WEATHER SONG

Sung to: "BINGO"

        F   Bb   F
There was a time when we got wet

       F   C   F
   and rainy was the weather,

F Bb   F Bb   F Bb
R-A-I-N-Y, R-A-I-N-Y, R-A-I-N-Y,

       C   F
   and rainy was the weather.

        F   Bb   F
There was a time when we got hot

       F   C   F
   and sunny was the weather,

F Bb   F Bb   F Bb
S-U-N-N-Y, S-U-N-N-Y, S-U-N-N-Y,

       C   F
   and sunny was the weather.

       F   Bb   F
There was a time when we got cold

       F   C   F
   and snowy was the weather.

F Bb   F Bb   F Bb
S-N-O-W-Y, S-N-O-W-Y, S-N-O-W-Y,

       C   F
   and snowy was the weather.

       F   Bb   F
There was a time when we were blown

       F   C   F
   and windy was the weather.

F Bb   F Bb   F Bb
W-I-N-D-Y, W-I-N-D-Y, W-I-N-D-Y,

       C   F
   and windy was the weather.

Sister Linda Kaman R.S.M.
Pittsburgh, PA

RAIN, RAIN FALLING DOWN

Sung to: "Row, Row, Row Your Boat"

C   C
Rain, rain falling down,
   (Wiggle fingers downward)
C   C
Falling on the ground.

C   C
Pitter, patter, pitter, patter,

G   C
What a lovely (squishy, noisy, silly, etc.) sound.

Susan A. Miller
Kutztown, PA

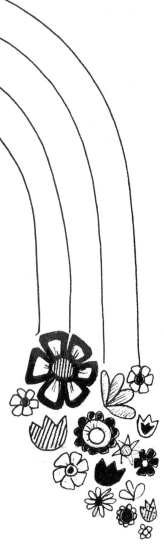

OH RAINBOW, OH RAINBOW

Sung to: "Oh, Christmas Tree"

G   D   G
Oh, rainbow, Oh, rainbow

    Am   D G
How lovely are your colors.

G   D   G
Oh, rainbow, Oh, rainbow

    Am   D G
How lovely are your colors,

G   C
Purple, red and orange too,

D7   G
Yellow, green, and blue so true.

    G   E7
Oh, rainbow, Oh, rainbow

    Am   D7 G
How lovely are your colors.

Stella Waldron
Lincoln, NE

ZIM BAM

Sung to: "Twinkle, Twinkle Little Star

C   C   F   C
Zim bam, zim bam, zim bam bee

   G7   C   G7   C
I see a rainbow over the tree.

C   G7   C   G7
Zim bam, zim bam, zim bam bay

   C   G7   C G7
I see a rainbow far away.

C   C   F   C
Zim bam, zim bam, zim bam by

   G7   C   G7   C
I see a rainbow in the sky.

C   C   F   C
Zim bam, zim bam, zim bam boo

   G7   C   G7 C
I see a rainbow over you.

Jean Warren

28

MARCH 17th

Sung to: "Row, Row, Row Your Boat"

   C   C
I like this day March 17th.

   C   C
I like the good St. Pat.

    C   C
He loved the land called Ireland.

    G7   C
Now, what do you think of that?

   C   C
I like this day March 17th.

   C   C
I like the good St. Pat.

    C   C
He drove the snakes right from the land.

    G7   C
Now, what do you think of that?

   C   C
I like this day March 17th.

   C   C
I like the good St. Pat.

    C   C
He taught the people to be good.

    G7   C
Now, what do you think of that?

   C   C
I like this day March 17th.

   C   C
I like the good St. Pat.

    C   C
He used the shamrock growing green.

    G7   C
Now, what do you think of that?

   C   C
I like this day March 17th.

   C   C
I like the good St. Pat.

    C   C
So we'll help the Irish celebrate.

    G7   C
Now, what do you think of that?

NOTE: Legend has it that St. Patrick freed Ireland of snakes. He taught the people by illustrating truths with the shamrock.

Betty Ruth Baker
Waco, TX

LEPRECHAUNS

Sung to: "Three Blind Mice"

C   G   C   C   G   C
Leprechauns, Leprechauns,

C G7 C   C G7 C
Hiding here, hiding there,

         C   G   C
They don't want us to see them play,

C   G   C
Every year on St. Patrick's Day.

C   G   C
See them smile in their cute little way,

C   G   C   C   G   C
Leprechauns, Leprechauns.

Dr. Margery A. Kranyik
Hyde Park, MA

DO YOU KNOW WHAT A SHAMROCK IS?

Sung to: "Mary Had A Little Lamb"

```
C                         C
Do you know what a shamrock is,

       G              C
   A shamrock is, a shamrock is,
C                         C
Do you know what a shamrock is?

      G            C
   A shamrock is a plant.


C                            C
Do you know where a shamrock grows,

       G                  C
   A shamrock grows, a shamrock grows,
C                            C
Do you know where a shamrock grows?

      G                       C
   A shamrock grows on (in) the ground.


C                              C
Do you know what color a shamrock is,

       G              C
   A shamrock is, a shamrock is,
C                              C
Do you know what color a shamrock is?

      G            C
   A shamrock is green.
```

June L. Haggard
Lake Geneva, WI

I'M A LITTLE LEPRECHAUN

Sung to: "I'm A Little Teapot"

```
C
I'm a little leprechaun.

F        C
Can you see?

G7     C  G7       C
I'm as tiny as I can be.

  C              C      F   C
I only come around just once a year.

F              C      G  G7 C
That's when St. Patrick's Day is near.
```

Betty Ruth Baker
Waco, TX

LEPRECHAUN'S MARCH

Sung to: "Twinkle, Twinkle Little Star"

```
C                  F      C
Leprechauns are marching by,

G7         C       G7       C
See how cute they wink their eye.

C         G7       C      G7
See them marching two by two,

C         G7         C      G7
Can't you see them wave to you,

C                    F      C
I think St. Patrick's Day is near,

   G7      C    G7          C
Because the Leprechauns are here.
```

Dr. Margery A. Kranyik
Hyde Park, MA

DID YOU EVER SEE A BUNNY?

Sung to: "Did You Ever See a Lassie"

       F   F   C   F
Did you ever see a bunny, a bunny, a bunny

       F   F   C   F
Did you ever see a bunny, munching his lunch.

  C7   F   C7   F
He munches and crunches, and munches and crunches

       F   F   C7   F
Did you ever see a bunny, munching his lunch?

       F   F   C   F
Did you ever see a bunny, a bunny, a bunny

       F   F   C   F
Did you ever see a bunny wiggle his nose?

  C7   F   C7   F
He wiggles and giggles, and wiggles and giggles

       F   F   C7   F
Did you ever see a bunny wiggle his nose?

       F   F   C   F
Did you ever see a bunny, a bunny, a bunny

       F   F   C   F
Did you ever see a bunny flap his big ears?

  C7   F   C7   F
He flips them and flaps them and flips them and flaps them

       F   F   C7   F
Did you ever see a bunny flap his big ears?

       F   F   C   F
Did you ever see a bunny, a bunny, a bunny

       F   F   C   F
Did you ever see a bunny hop down the lane?

  C7   F   C7   F
He hips and hops and hips and hops

       F   F   C7   F
Did you ever see a bunny hop down the lane?

Jean Warren

EASTER BUNNY

Sung to: "Twinkle, Twinkle Little Star"

C   F   C
Easter Bunny, soft and white,

G7   C   G7   C
Hopping quickly out of sight.

C   F   C   G7
Thank you for the eggs you bring,

        C   F   C   G7
At Easter time we welcome spring

C   F   C
Easter Bunny, soft and white,

G7   C   G7   C
Hopping quickly out of sight.

Irmgard Fuertges
Kitchner, Ontario

THE GARDEN SONG

Sung to: "Row, Row, Row Your Boat"

C   C
Dig, dig, dig your garden

C   C
Make it smooth and neat,

C
Push, push, push that shovel,

G   C
Push it with your feet.

C   C
Plant, plant, plant your seeds

C   C
Push them down an inch

C   C
Cover your seeds with some soil

G   C
Cover with a pinch.

C   C
Water, water, water your seeds

C   C
This will help them sprout,

C   C
Sprinkle lightly and let's not pour

     G   C
And don't let them dry out.

C   C
Sun, sun, sunshine

C   C
It will turn them green,

C   C
Carrots and radishes and peppers, too

     G   C
Tomatoes and some beans.

C   C
Watch, watch, watch them grow

C
See them grow so tall

C   C
Put a scarecrow in the ground

G
To protect them all.

THE SEED

Sung to: "Twinkle, Twinkle Little Star"

C   F   C
I'm a little planted seed.

G7   C   G7   C
See the rain falling on me.

C   F   C   G7
Sun shines down through the trees.

C   F   C   G7
These are the things I need indeed.

C   F   C
Oh, how happy they make me.

G7   C   G7   C
I'm a little growing seed.

Adele Engelbracht
River Ridge, LA

C   C
Pull, pull, pull the weeds

C   C
Keep your garden clear

        C
To make them grow up and out

       G   C
And stretch out here and there.

C   C
Pick, pick, pick your feast

C   C
Cook some veggie soup

C   C
You'll have lots and lots to eat,

     G   C
Enough to feed the group.

Kathleen M. Todd
North Wales, PA

SONGS ABOUT SUMMER

IT IS SUMMER

Sung to: "Frere Jacques"

C   C
It is summer, it is summer

C   C
Lots of fun, lots of fun,

C
Sun is shining on me

C
Sun is shining on me.

C   C
I'll have fun. I'll have fun.

Saundra Winnett
Fort Worth, TX

ON THE FIRST DAY OF SUMMER

Sung to: "Twelve Days of Christmas"

| | F | | Dm | | Gm | ` | C | | F | | Bb | | F | G | F |
On the first day of summer, my true love gave to me a robin in a maple tree.

                  F   Dm
On the second day of summer . . .

               F   Dm
On the third day of summer . . .

                F   Dm
On the fourth day of summer . . .

                F   Dm
On the fifth day of summer . . .

                F   Dm
On the sixth day of summer . . .

                F   Dm
On the seventh day of summer . . .

                F   Dm
On the eighth day of summer . . .

                F   Dm
On the ninth day of summer . . .

                F   Dm
On the tenth day of summer . . .

                F   Dm
On the eleventh day of summer . . .

                F   Dm
On the twelfth day of summer . . .

C   Bb
2 ducks a-waddling

Bb
3 bees a-buzzin

F Bb
4 watermelons

Am G7   C
5 picnic baskets

F Gm
6 wormy apples

F   Gm
7 ants a-marchin

F   Gm
8 swimmers swimming

F   Gm
9 children playing

F   Gm
10 flowers blooming

F   Gm
11 mowers mowing

F   Gm
12 gardens growing

Suzanne L. Harrington & Wendy Spaide
North Wales, PA

BRIGHT SUN

Sung to: "Row, Row, Row Your Boat"

C   C
Bright sun shining down,
  (Spread fingers and move slowly downward)
C   C
Shining on the ground.
C   C
What a lovely face you have,
  (Make a large circle in front of face with arms)
G   C
Yellow, big and round.

Susan A. Miller
Kutztown, PA

SING A SONG OF SUNSHINE

Sung to: "Sing a Song of Sixpence"

G   G
Sing a song of sunshine

 D   D
Be happy every day.

 D   D
Sing a song of sunshine

    G   G
You'll chase the clouds away.

  G   G
Be happy every moment

 C
No matter what you do

   D
Just sing and sing and sing and sing

       G
And let the sunshine through.

Jean Warren

HAPPY FATHER'S DAY

Sung to: "Oh Christmas Tree"

G
Oh, Father's Day

DG
Oh, Father's Day

Am$$D7G
What a grand day it is.

G
Oh, Father's Day

DG
Oh, Father's Day

AmD7G
Honor Dad with love.

GC
Give him hugs

D7
Love him true

D7$$G
Honor him with special You.

G
Oh, Father's Day

DG
Oh, Father's Day

AmD7G
How we love you true!

AmD7$$G
We love you - yes we do!

Kristine Wagoner
Pacific, WA

WHERE IS DADDY?

Sung to: "Frere Jacques"

F
Where is Daddy?

F
Where is Daddy?

F
He's at work.

F
He's at work.

F
Hurry up and come home.

F
Hurry up and come home.

F
We miss you.

F
We miss you.

Substitute other names for Daddy if you wish and let
your children sing about other people they miss.

Diane Alifano
Poway, CA

36

HAPPY BIRTHDAY TO AMERICA

Sung to: "Oh, Christmas Tree"

    G
America

D G
America

Am   D7   G
Happy Birthday to You

    G
America

D G
America

Am   D7   G
It's your birthday too

    G
We celebrate

      C
Your birthday

    D7
By fireworks

      G
And picnics too

D G
America

D G
America

Am   D7   G
How we love you true.

Am   D7   G
We-e love you, yes we do.

Kristine Wagoner
Pacific, WA

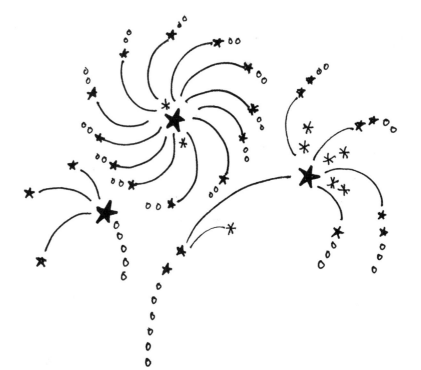

AMERICAN FLAG

Sung to: "Frere Jacques"

C   C
What is red, what is white

C   C
What is blue, what is striped?

C   C
What has many stars, what has many stars,

C   C
Can you guess, how many there are?

Saundra Winnett
Fort Worth, TX

AUGUST

Sung to: "The More We Get Together"

    C   G   C
Oh, sing a song of August, of August, of August,

    C   C   G   C
Oh, Sing a song of August, bright summer is here.

    G   C   G   C
We wear suntan lotion and go to the ocean,

    C   C   G   C
Oh, sing a song of August, bright summer is here.

(Make up other verses about summer fun.)

Mildred Hoffman
Tacoma, WA

SWIMMING

Sung to: "Sailing, Sailing"

F
Swimming, swimming   (move arms as if swimming)

Bb   F
In our swimming hole   (make circle with hands)

    Bb
When days are hot   (wipe brow)

    F
When days are cold   (hug self as if shivering)

Bb   C
In our swimming hole   (make circle with hands)

F
Breast stroke, side stroke   (imitate swimming stroke)

Bb   F
Fancy diving, too!   (pretend to dive)

    Bb   F
Oh, don't you wish you never had

Bb   C   F
Anything else to do but . . .

    (Repeat entire song)

Jean Anderson
Saint Paul, MN

SONGS ABOUT FALL

LEAVES ARE FALLING 'ROUND THE TOWN

Sung to: "Twinkle, Twinkle Little Star"

C   C   F   C
Leaves are falling 'round the town

G7   C   G7   C
Watch them fall right on the ground

C   G7   C   G7
Autumn's coming, it is true

C   G7   C   G7
Then comes winter just for you

C   C   F   C
Leaves are falling 'round the town

  G7   C   G7   C
Falling, falling all around.

Judy Hall
Wytheville, VA

LEAVES, LEAVES FALLING DOWN

Sung to: "Row, Row, Row Your Boat"

C   C
Leaves, leaves falling down,
   (Wiggle fingers downward)
C   C
Falling on the ground.

C   C
Red, Yellow, Orange and Brown,

G   C
Triangle, oval and round.
   (With each thumb touching and each forefinger
    touching, make shapes.)

Susan A. Miller
Kutztown, PA

FOUR SEASONS

Sung to: "Twinkle, Twinkle Little Star"

C   F   C
Flowers, swimming, pumpkins, snow

G7   C   G7   C
Make the seasons we all know.

C   F   C   G7
Every year they are the same

C   F   C   G7
And we give them each a name.

C   F   C
Summer, Fall, Winter, Spring

G7   C   G7   C
Count the seasons as we sing.

Mrs. Bill Dean
Richland, WA

WINTER, SPRING, SUMMER, FALL

Sung to: "This Old Man"

C   C
Winter, Spring, Summer, Fall

F   G7
There are seasons, four in all

C   C
Weather changes, sun and rain and snow

G7   C G7 C
Leaves fall down and flowers grow.

C   C
Winter, Spring, Summer, Fall

F   G7
There are seasons, four in all

C   C
Look outside and you will see

G7   C G7 C
Just what season it will be!

Judy Hall
Wytheville, VA

SUMMER, FALL, WINTER, SPRING

Sung to: "Old MacDonald Had a Farm"

C   C   F   C
Summer, fall, winter, spring.

C   G7   C
Sun, leaves, snow and rain.

         C   C   F   C
And if you watch you will see,

        C   G7   C
seasons change again.

          C
With a sun shine here,

         C
a snow flake there

C   C   C   C
rain and leaves fall everywhere.

C   C   F   C
Summer, fall, winter, spring.

C   G7   C
Sun, leaves, snow and rain.

Saundra Winnett
Fort Worth, TX

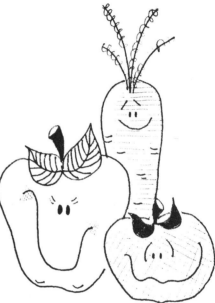

APPLE SONG

Sung to: "Have You Ever Seen A Lassie?"

        C   C   G7   C
Have you ever seen an apple, an apple, an apple,

        C   C   G7   C
Have you ever seen an apple, that grows on a tree?

 G7   C   G7   C
A red one, a yellow one, a red one, a yellow one.

        C   C   G7   C
Have you ever seen an apple, that grows on a tree?

Darla Carson
Ellinwood, KS

AUTUMN LEAVES ALL AROUND ME

Sung to: "Mary Had A Little Lamb"

C
Autumn leaves - - - All around me

                        C

G
All around me

G
All around me

C
Autumn leaves - - - All around me

      G   C
What colors do you see?

C
Red and Yellow, Gold and Brown

G
Gold and Brown

C
Gold and Brown

C
Red and Yellow, Gold and Brown

G   C
Falling gracefully.

Susan Paprocki
Elmhurst, IL

HARVEST TIME

Sung to: "Twinkle, Twinkle Little Star"

C   F   C
Harvest Time is here again

G7   C   G7   C
In the garden we must dig

C   F   C   G7
Carrots, radishes, onions too

C   F   C   G7
All so fresh and yummy too.

C   F   C
Harvest Time is here again

G7   C   G7   C
Won't be long till Fall is here.

Kristine Wagoner
Pacific, WA

AUTUMN LEAVES

Sung to: "Mary Had A Little Lamb"

C   C
Autumn leaves are falling down,

G7   C
Falling down, falling down.

C   C
Autumn leaves are falling down.

G7   C
Yellow, red and brown.

C   C
Rake them up as they fall down,

      G7   C
As they fall down, as they fall down.

C   C
Rake them up as they fall down.

G7   C
Yellow, red and brown.

C   C
Here comes the wind on a windy day,

      G7   C
A windy day, a windy day.

C   C
Here comes the wind on a windy day.

      G7   C
And blows them all away.

(Children can cut out paper leaves in art and dramatize the song. A child may be the wind.)

Betty Ruth Baker
Waco, TX

THE LEAVES OF THE TREES

Sung to: "The Wheels on the Bus"

          C   G7
The leaves of the trees turn orange and red

    G7   C
orange and red, orange and red

          C   G7
The leaves of the trees turn orange and red

    G7   C
All through the town.

          C   G7
The leaves of the trees come tumbling down

    G7   C
tumbling down, tumbling down

          C   G7
The leaves of the trees come tum...

    G7   C
All through the town.

          C
The leaves on the ground g...

    G7   C
Swish, swish, swish,   s...

          C
The leaves on the grou...   sh

    G7   C
All through the to...

LEAVES ARE FALLING

Sung to: "Mary Had A Little Lamb"

C   C
Leaves are falling to the ground,

   G   C
to the ground, to the ground,

C
Leaves are falling to the ground,

G   C
Pretty autumn leaves.

C   C
C'mon boys let's rake them up

   G   C
rake them up, rake them up,

C   C
C'mon girls let's rake them up,

G   C
Pretty autumn leaves.

C   C
C'mon all, let's pile them high,

   G   C
pile them high, pile them high,

C   C
C'mon all, let's pile them high,

G   C
Pretty autumn leaves.

C   C
Now let's jump into the pile,

   G   C
into the pile, into the pile,

C   C
Now let's jump into the pile,

   G   C
Of pretty autumn leaves.

Bonnie Harrison
Princeton Junction, NJ

THE LEAVES ARE FALLING DOWN

Sung to: "Farmer In The Dell"

        C   C
The leaves are falling down,

        C   C
The leaves are falling down

C   C
School is here and fall is near

        C   G
The leaves are falling down.

        C   C
The leaves are falling down,

        C   C
The leaves are falling down

C   C
Some are red and some are brown

        C   G   C
The leaves are falling down.

        C   C
The leaves are falling down,

        C   C
The leaves are falling down

        C   C
They tickle your nose and touch your toes

        C   G   C
The leaves are falling down.

June L. Haggard
Lake Geneva, WI

COLUMBUS

Sung to: "Mary Had A Little Lamb"

C ... C
Columbus sailed the ocean blue,

G7 ... C
Ocean blue, ocean blue.

C ... C
Columbus sailed the ocean blue,

G7 ... C
To find this land for me and you.

C ... C
Columbus sailed the ocean blue,

G7 ... C
Ocean blue, ocean blue.

C ... C
Columbus sailed the ocean blue,

G7 ... C
In fourteen hundred ninety-two.

C ... C
Three ships he used to sail the sea,

G7 ... C
Sail the sea, sail the sea.

C ... C
Three ships he used to sail the sea,

G7 ... C
The Pinta, Nina and Santa Maria.

C ... C
At last some land came to view,

G7 ... C
Came to view, came to view.

C ... C
At last some land came to view,

G7 ... C
In fourteen hundred ninety-two.

Betty Ruth Baker
Waco, TX

I'M A JACK O' LANTERN

Sung to: "I'm a Little Teapot"

C
I'm a Jack o' lantern

F ... C
Look at me!

G7 ... C ... G7 ... C
I'm as happy as I can be.

C ... G7
Put a candle in and

C ... G7
Light the light.

C ... G7 ... C ... G7 ... C
I'll scare you because it's Halloween night.

C
Boo -- oo -- oo !!!

Betty Ruth Baker
Waco, TX

44

HAVE YOU SEEN . . . ?

Sung to: "The Muffin Man"

F   F
Have you seen the pumpkin man,

    G7   C
The pumpkin man, the pumpkin man,

F   F
Have you seen the pumpkin man,

    G7   C   F
Who lives in the pumpkin patch?

F   F
Have you seen the old black witch,

    G7   C
The old black witch, the old black witch,

F   F
Have you seen the old black witch,

    G7   C   F
Who lives in the haunted house?

F   F
Have you seen the scary ghost,

    G7   C
The scary ghost, the scary ghost,

F   F
Have you seen the scary ghost,

    G7   C   F
Who lives in the old ghost town?

F   F
Have you seen the big black bat,

    G7   C
The big black bat, the big black bat,

F   F
Have you seen the big black bat,

    G7   C   F
Who lives in the cold dark cave?

F   F
Yes, we have. We've seen these things.

G7   C
Seen these things, seen these things,

F   F
Yes, we have, we've seen these things,

    G7   C   F
We saw them on Halloween!

1983 - 1984 Kindergarten Class
National Child Care Center No. 1002
Glendale, AZ

MR. PUMPKIN

Sung to: "Frere Jacques"

F   F
Mr. Pumpkin, Mr. Pumpkin.   (Hands around head)

F   F
Eyes so round, eyes so round.   (Circle two fingers for eyes)

F   F
Halloween is coming, Halloween is coming.   (Pointer fingers on
each hand going
back and forth)

F   F
To my town, to my town.

Susan Paprocki
Elmhurst, IL

SOMETIMES I LIKE TO WALK IN THE DARK

Sung to: "Pop Goes the Weasel"

     F   C   F   F
Sometimes I like to walk in the dark.

  F   C   F
I like to shout and scream.

  F   C   F
I sneak behind somebody I know

Bb   C   F
BOO!   It's Halloween.

Frank Dally
Akeny, IA

GHOSTS AND WITCHES

Sung to: "Twinkle, Twinkle Little Star"

C   C   F   C
Ghosts and witches, goblins too!

G7   C   G7   C
Halloween is just for you

C G7   C   G7
Everyone dressed up today

C   G7   C   G7
Trick or treaters on the way

C   C   F   C
But be careful what you do

G7   C   G7
One of them might scare you   (say slower)

C
BOO!   (children yell)

Judy Hall
Wytheville, VA

GHOSTS AND GOBLINS

Sung to: "Frere Jacques"

C   C
Ghosts and goblins, ghosts and goblins,

C   C
All around, all around

C   C
Witches on their broomsticks, witches on their broomsticks

C   C
Halloween, Halloween.

Frank Dally
Akeny, IA

46

THANKSGIVING DAY

Sung to: "Old MacDonald Had a Farm"

      F   Bb   F
Thanksgiving Day, will soon be here,

F   C7   F
Let us now give thanks.

F   Bb   F
For the blessings of the year,

F   C7   F
Let us now give thanks.

        F
With a thankful heart.

        F
With a thankful heart.

    F   F   F
Thanksgiving Day, we'll stop to say,

F   Bb   F
For the blessings of the year,

F   C7   F
We now give thanks.

Betty Ruth Baker
Waco, TX

LET US GIVE THANKS

Sung to: "Here We Go Round the Mulberry Bush"

          F
Thanksgiving Day will soon be here,

C7
Soon be here, soon be here.

          F
Thanksgiving Day will soon be here.

C7   F
Let us now give thanks.

F
For the blessings of the year,

C7
Of the year, of the year.

F
For the blessings of the year.

C7   F
Let us now give thanks.

F
For our homes we love so dear,

C7
Love so dear, love so dear.

F
For our homes we love so dear.

C7   F
Let us now give thanks.

Betty Ruth Baker
Waco, TX

TO GRANDMA'S HOUSE

Sung to: "Over the River and Through the Woods"

C   C
Over the river and through the woods

    F   C
To Grandma's house we go.

     Dm   G7
The car knows the way

   C   Am
To go today

    D7   G
To Grandma's house. Hoo-ray ay!

C   C
Over the river and through the woods

    F   C
To Grandma's house we go.

    F   B7
To play with the toys

      C   Am
And make lots of noise

     C   G7   C
And give Grandma a kiss! (kiss sound!)

M.M. Gaspar
Byfield, MA

SMELLS LIKE THANKSGIVING

Sung to: "Frere Jacques"

F   F
Smells like Thanksgiving, smells like Thanksgiving

F   F
Mmmm so good, mmmm so good

F   F
I can smell the turkey, I can smell the pies

F   F
Mmmm so good, mmmm so good.

Jean Warren

MR. TURKEY

Sung to: "Frere Jacques"

C   C
Mr. Turkey, Mr. Turkey,

C   C
Run away. Run away.

C
If you are not careful,

C
You will be a mouthful,

     C   C   C
Thanksgiving Day, Thanksgiving Day.

Dr. Margery A. Kranyik
Hyde Park, MA

SONGS ABOUT SCHOOL

LITTLE CHILDREN

Sung to: "Twinkle, Twinkle Little Star"

```
C            F      C
Little children how are you?

G7      C    G7        C
Keep a smile all day through.


C          F       C          G7
Come to school to dance and play.

C        F    C          G7
Paint a picture of your day.


C            F      C
Little children sing along.

G7      C    G7        C
Keep a smile all day long.
```

Carolyn Arey
Salisbury, NC

49

WELCOME, WELCOME

Sung to: "Twinkle, Twinkle Little Star"

C
Welcome, welcome,

    F   C
    All my friends.

    F   C
We'll learn you name

    G   C
    Through this game.

C   F   C   G
Annie, Annie it's your turn (insert name)

    C   F   C G C
    Take a block, and then return.

> The children sit in a circle with blocks in the center (or anything else, name tags if the children can identify their name). Repeat the song with the next child's name.

Susan Paprocki
Elmhurst, IL

HI SONG

Sung to: "Oh Dear, What Can the Matter Be?"

A clown puppet or a Sesame Street character would be just right to sing this song, which uses childrens' names and describes their clothing.

C
Hi, ___(Mary)___, who is your playmate there,   (Insert name)

G
Hi, _____, who is your playmate there,

C
Hi, _____, who is your playmate there,

G   C
Wearing the red jogging suit?

(Mary answers child's name, "Billy" and the puppet now sings:)

C
Hi, ___(Billy)___, who is your playmate there, (etc.)

G   C
Wearing the strawberry dress?

Mildred Hoffman
Tacoma, WA

DAY SONG

Sung to: "Skip To My Lou"

C   C
Hey, hey what do you say

G7   G7
Hey, hey what do you say

C   C
Hey, hey what do you say

G7   C
For today's a _____ day.

C   C
Hey, hey let's join hands

G7   G7
Hey, hey let's join hands

C   C
Hey, hey let's join hands

G7   C
While we sit and make our plans.

C   C
Hey, hey what do you say

G7   G7
Hey, hey what do you say

C   C
Hey, hey what do you say

G7   C
For today's a _____ day.

Fill in blanks with whatever type of day it is:

good-day	Mon-day	red-day
new-day	Tues-day	blue-day
sunny-day	Wednes-day	round-day
birth-day	Thurs-day	square-day
holi-day	Fri-day	etc.

Jean Warren

TODAY IS

Sung to: "Mary Had A Little Lamb"

      F   F   C   F
Today is _____ day, _____ day, _____ day,

      F   F   C   F
Today is _____ day, let's all sing a song.

F   F   C   F
It will be a fun day, fun day, fun day,

F   F   C   F
It will be a fun day, all day long.

F   F   C   F
Sing a song of _____ day, _____ day, _____ day,

F   F   C   F
Sing a song of _____ day, all day long.

Change the word in the blank to fit the day.

Examples: Mon-day, Tues-day, etc.
            Sunny-day, Windy-day, etc.
            Birth-day, Holi-day, Valentine's-day
            Blue-day, red-day, etc.

Jean Warren

BIRTHDAY SONG

Sung to: "Oh, What A Beautiful Morning"

C   Bb   F
Oh, what a special morning

C   G7
Oh, what a special day

C   F   Fdim.
It's _____ _____'s birthday

C   G7   C
We wish (him/her) the best today.

(Fill in birthday child's name in the blank.)

Jean Warren

I AM TURNING

Sung to: "Frere Jacques"

F   F
I am turning, I am turning,

F   F
Round and round, round and round

F
First I go one way

F
Then I go the other way

F   F
Touch the ground, now sit down.

Susan Widdifield
Poulsbo, WA

Additional Verses:

   I am dancing

   I am marching

   I am chugging

   I am flying

   I am moving

   I am spinning

WE ALL LIKE TO DANCE AND SING

Sung to: "Mary Had A Little Lamb"

C   C
We all like to dance and sing,

   G   C
Dance and sing, dance and sing,

C   C
We all like to dance and sing,

   G   C
Tra, la, la, la, la.

(Move body to tune and sing.)

Saundra Winnett
Fort Worth, TX

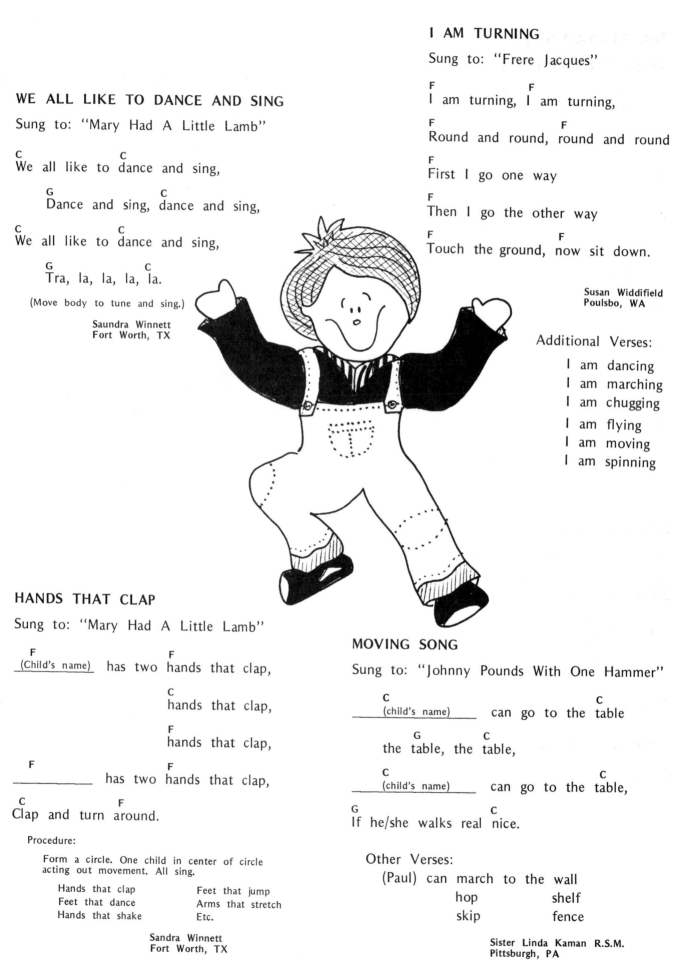

HANDS THAT CLAP

Sung to: "Mary Had A Little Lamb"

  F   F
(Child's name) has two hands that clap,

                  C
              hands that clap,

                  F
              hands that clap,

  F   F
_____ has two hands that clap,

C   F
Clap and turn around.

Procedure:

   Form a circle. One child in center of circle
   acting out movement. All sing.

     Hands that clap   Feet that jump
     Feet that dance   Arms that stretch
     Hands that shake   Etc.

Sandra Winnett
Fort Worth, TX

MOVING SONG

Sung to: "Johnny Pounds With One Hammer"

        C   C
_____ can go to the table
(child's name)

        G   C
    the table, the table,

        C   C
_____ can go to the table,
(child's name)

G   C
If he/she walks real nice.

Other Verses:

   (Paul) can march to the wall

         hop   shelf

         skip   fence

Sister Linda Kaman R.S.M.
Pittsburgh, PA

THE SHAPE-UP SONG

Sung to: "Farmer in the Dell"

     C   C
We're jumping up and down

     C   C
We're jumping up and down

     C   C
We're getting lots of exercise

     C   G   C
We're jumping up and down.

2nd verse . . .   We bend and touch our toes . . .

3rd   . . .   We kick our legs up high . . .

4th   . . .   We jog around the room . . .

5th   . . .   We wiggle our whole body . . .

6th   . . .   We stretch up to the sky . . .

Suzanne L. Harrington & Wendy Spaide
North Wales, PA

STRETCHING, STRETCHING BOYS AND GIRLS

Sung to: "Twinkle, Twinkle Little Star"

C   F   C
Stretching, stretching boys and girls,

G7   C   G7   C
Show the world who you are,

 C   G7   C   G7
Reach above the moon and stars

 C   G7   C   G7
Show the world who you are.

 C   F   C
Stretching, stretching boys and girls,

G7   C   G7   C
Reach above the moon and stars.

Saundra Winnett
Fort Worth, TX

I CAN BEND AND TOUCH THE FLOOR

Sung to: "Mary Had a Little Lamb"

F   F
I can bend and touch the floor,

     C   F
touch the floor, touch the floor.

F   F
Put your hands on the floor,

   C   F
Now let's walk around.

Saundra Winnett
Fort Worth, TX

STRETCH, STRETCH, STRETCH YOUR ARMS

Sung to: "Row, Row, Row Your Boat"

 C   C
Stretch, stretch, stretch your arms

 C   C
High above your head,

 C
Stretch so high,

 C
Reach the sky,

      G   C
And then we'll stretch again.

(Children stretch high as they can while singing.)

Saundra Winnett
Fort Worth, TX

53

TRIP SONG

Sung to: "Mary Had A Little Lamb"

C
_____ took a trip one day

G7   C
trip one day, trip one day

C   C
_____ took a trip one day

G7   C
and tell us what you did!

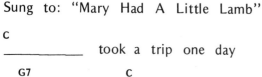

C   C
She helped Grandpa on the farm

G7   C
On the farm, On the farm

C   C
She helped Grandpa on the farm

G7   C
Doing farm work!

Other Suggestions:

He helped grandma bake some cookies, etc.
    (Then ate them all up)

She rode on lots of rides
    (At Disneyland)

Let your children tell about a trip they took, and let everyone sing about their trip.

Judy Hall
Wytheville, VA

JIMMY JONES BUILT A CAR

Sung to: "Old MacDonald Had a Farm"

C   F   C
_____ _____built a car

C   G   C
E I E I O

             C   F   C
And on this car he put some _____

C   G   C
E I E I O

        C   C
With a _____ here and a _____ there

C   C
Here a _____ there a_____

C   C
Everywhere a _____ , _____

C   F   C
'_____ _____ built a car

C   G   C
E I E I O

Jean Warren

Sing the song, putting in the name of a different child each time. Let the child decide what it is he or she is going to build. Also let them name the specific items they will use for different verses of the song. Examples for car song: wheels, horn, lights, etc... Examples of other items children might want to build: a house, a garden, a fire engine, a school, a playground, etc.

WHEN WE WALK DOWN THE STAIRS

Sung to: "Turkey in the Straw"

     C   C
When we walk down the stairs we walk next to the wall.

   C   G
We hold on to the handrail, so we won't fall.

   C   C
We never push or shove because it's not the thing to do.

   C   G   C
We walk the stairs so carefully and hope that you do too.

Frank Dally
Ankeny, IA

WHO'S TALKING?

Sung to: "London Bridge"

C   C
When you listen to a voice

G   C
You can tell whose it is.

C
Everybody close their eyes.

G   C
Guess who's talking.

One person talks and each person in the
group takes turns trying to guess whose
voice it was.

Frank Dally
Ankeny, IA

LOOK AT ME AND REMEMBER

Sung to: "Frere Jacques"

F   F
Look at me, look at me,

F   F
Remember me, remember me,

F   F
What am I wearing? What am I wearing?

F   F
Look at me, look at me.

Saundra Winnett
Fort Worth, TX

SEVEN DAYS IN A WEEK

Sung to: "For He's A Jolly Good Fellow"

      F   Bb F C   F
Oh, there's seven days in a week, seven days in a week,

F   Bb   F   Bb C F
Seven days in a week, and I can say them all.

F   Bb F C
Sunday, Monday, and Tuesday, Wednesday, Thursday, and   F
Friday,

F   Bb   F   Bb   F
Saturday is the last day, and I can say them all.

Darla Carson
Ellinwood, KS

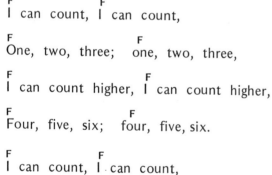

I CAN COUNT

Sung to: "Frere Jacques"

F   F
I can count, I can count,

F   F
One, two, three; one, two, three,

F   F
I can count higher, I can count higher,

F   F
Four, five, six; four, five, six.

F   F
I can count, I can count,

F   F
One, two, three, four, five, six

F   F
I can count higher, I can count higher,

F   F
Seven, eight, nine; seven, eight, nine.

Etc. . . .

Saundra Winnett
Fort Worth, TX

COUNT THE DAYS

Sung to: "Twinkle, Twinkle Little Star"

C   C   F   C
Come along and count with me

G7   C   G7   C
There are seven days you see.

C   G7   C   G7
Monday, Tuesday, Wednesday too,

C   G7   C   G7
Thursday, Friday — just for you,

C   C   F   C
Saturday, Sunday — that's the end

G7   C   G7   C
Now let's sing it all again!

Judy Hall
Wytheville, VA

ONE — TWO — THREE

Sung to: "This Old Man"

C
One — two — three

C
Count with me

F   G7
It's as easy as can be —

C   C
Four, five, six, seven-eight, nine, ten

G7   C   G7 C
Now let's start it once again.

Judy Hall
Wytheville, VA

OPPOSITES

Sung to: "Mary Had A Little Lamb"

C   G   C
Up and down are opposites, opposites, opposites;

C   G   C
Up and down are opposites, that we learned today.

(Use hand motions where possible, or actions, and see how many
opposites you can sing about.)

SUGGESTIONS: Hard & Soft   Big & Little
               Black & White   Etc.

Lynn Beaird
Lompoc, CA

COLOR SONG

Sung to: "Twinkle, Twinkle Little Star"
              (Using first 4 measures only)

C   F   C
Put your *red shape in the air

G7   C   G7   C
Hold it high and leave it there.

C   F   C   G7
Put your red shape on your back

C   F   C   G7
Now please lay it in your lap.

C   F   C
Hold your red shape in your hand

G7   C   G7   C
Now will everyone please stand.

C   F   C   G7
Wave your red shape at the door

C   F   C   G7
Now please lay it on the floor.

C   F   C
Hold your red shape and jump, jump, jump

G7   C   G7   C
Throw your red shape way, way up.

*Substitute different colors. (Cut several shapes from
different colors of construction paper. Great for
recognizing colors, shapes, and direction.)

Trish Peckham
Raleigh, NC

HAVE YOU EVER HAD AN APPLE?

Sung to: "Have You Ever Seen A Lassie?"

       C   C   G   C
Have you ever had an apple, an apple, an apple?

       C
Have you ever had an apple

 G   C
And heard it go "crunch"?

       C   C   G   C
Have you ever had an orange, an orange, an orange?

       C   C
Have you ever had an orange

 G   C
And heard it go "slurp"?

       C   C   G   C
Have you ever had a banana, a banana, a banana?

       C   C
Have you ever had a banana

 G   C
And heard it go "mush"?

Frank Dally
Akeny, IA

WHAT IS GREEN AND RED — GUESSING GAME

Sung to: "Frere Jacques"

C
What is green?

C
What is red?

C
What is big?

C
What is round?

C
What has lots of seeds?

C
What is fun to eat?

C   C
Juicy treat, juicy treat.

Children sing and guess.
(Watermelon)

Saundra Winnett
Fort Worth, TX

SNACK SONG

Sung to: "Down By The Station"

F
Around our snack table

C   F
Early in the morning,

F
We get lots of good things

    C   F
    for our day.

F   C   F
Food we need to help us grow and play

F
Chew, chew, crunch, crunch,

C   F
Down it goes!

Sister Linda Kaman R.S.M.
Pittsburgh, PA

LUNCH IS ON THE WAY

LUNCH IS ON THE WAY

Sung to: The Farmer In The Dell"

     F   F
The lunch is on the way, the lunch is on the way,

                    F   C7   F
Heigh - o the derry - o, the lunch is on the way.

     F   F
We all will eat our food, we all will eat our food,

                    F   C   F
Heigh - o the derry - o, we all will eat our food.

     F   F
The food will help us grow, the food will help us grow.

F   F   C   F
Heigh - o the derry - o, the food will help us grow.

     F   F   C   F
And then we'll take our naps, and then we'll take our naps,

F   F   C   F
Heigh - o the derry - o, and then we'll take our naps.

     F   F
And we will grow some more, and we will grow some more,

F   F   C   F
Heigh - o the derry - o, and YES we will grow some more!

Pauline Laughter
Tulsa, OK

TELEPHONE SONGS

Sung to: "ABC Song"

C   F   C
7 4 3   7 9 8 2

G7   C   G7   C
That's what I'm supposed to do.

C   F   C   G7
7 4 3 yes, dial it true,

C   F C   G7
Now the 7 9 8 2

C   F   C
7 4 3   7 9 8 2

G7   C   G7   C
I am fine, how are you?

C   F   C
6 7 5, now I've begun

G7   C   G7   C
1 7 6 1, now I'm done.

C   F   C   G7
6 7 5 1 7 6 1

C   F   C   G7
Let's play outdoors in the sun.

C   F   C
6 7 5 1 7 6 1

G7   C   G7   C
Come to my house, we'll have fun.

Use the children's own telephone numbers. Put the number on a card and have the children read it when you hold it up at the appropriate place in the song. This strengthens the concept of reading from left to right, and trains in the memory of seven digits. The numbers repeated make a lilting chant-like song the children, and you, will enjoy.

Mildred Hoffman
Tacoma, WA

ALEXANDER GRAHAM BELL

Sung to: "Frere Jacques"

C
Alexander,

C
Alexander,

C
Graham Bell,

C
Graham Bell.

    C
He made something useful,

    C
He made something useful,

C   C
RING, RING, RING.

Children sing and guess.
(Telephone)

Saundra Winnett
Fort Worth, TX

THE HELPFUL "0" (ZERO)

Sung to: "Farmer in the Dell"

      C   C
The telephone is your friend,

      C   C
The telephone is your friend,

C   C
Hi, Ho the helpful "0",

      C   G7   C
The telephone is your friend.

      C   C
The telephone is not a toy!

      C   C
The telephone is not a toy!

C   C
Hi, Ho the helpful "0",

      C   G7   C
The telephone is not a toy.

      C   C
The telephone has a dial,

      C   C
The telephone has a dial,

C   C
Hi, Ho the helpful "0",

      C   G7   C
The telephone has a dial.

      C   C
The telephone has a receiver,

      C   C
The telephone has a receiver,

C   C
Hi, Ho the helpful "0",

      C   G7   C
The telephone has a receiver.

(Children can generate more verses
 of their own.)

Gail Ray
Fort Worth, TX

RING - A - LING - A - LING

Sung to: "Old MacDonald Had a Farm"

      C   F   C
The telephone is our good friend,

C   G   C
Ring-a-Ling-a-Ling.

      C   F   C
It helps us in emergencies,

C   G   C
Ring-a-Ling-a-Ling.

      C
With a ring-ring here,

      C
And a ring-ring there,

C
Here a ring.

C
There a ring.

C
Everywhere a ring-ring.

      C   F   C
The telephone is our good friend,

C   G   C
Ring-a-Ling-a-Ling.

Gail Ray
Fort Worth, TX

61

FIREFIGHTERS

Sung to: "Pop Goes The Weasel"

```
  C           G          C
Down the street the engine goes

      C        G         C
The firemen fight the fire

C       G        C
Up the ladder with their hose

F      G      C
Out goes the fire.
```

Mrs. Gary McNitt
Adrian, Michigan

I AM A FIREMAN

Sung to: "I'm A Little Teapot"

```
C          C        F        C
I am a fireman, dressed in red.

G7         C     G7      C
With my fire hat on my head.

C             C        F       C
I can drive the firetruck, fight fire too,

      F      C          G   G7  C
And help to make things safe for you.
```

Judy Hall
Wytheville, VA

I AM A POLICEMAN

Sung to: "I'm A Little Teapot"

```
C              F       C
I am a policeman, with my star.

G7      C      G7        C
I help people near and far.

C             C       F      C
If you have a problem, call on me.

      F      C      G  G7 C
And I will be there, 1, 2, 3!
```

Judy Hall
Wytheville, VA

62

PICKING UP THE BLOCKS

Sung to: "The Paw Paw Patch"

F   F
Picking up the blocks and put them on the shelf.

C   C
Picking up the blocks and put them on the shelf.

F   F
Picking up the blocks and put them on the shelf.

 C   F
Until our room is clean.

F   F
Thank you Johnny, you're a big help

C   C
Thank you Johnny, you're a big help

F   F
Thank you Johnny, you're a big help

C   F
Now our room is all cleaned up.

Jean Warren

CLEAN-UP TIME

Sung to: "Happy Birthday To You"

 F   C
It's time to clean (pick) up,

 C   F
It's time to clean up,

 F   Bb
It's time to clean u-up,

   F   C F
Put the toys on the shelf (in the box, in the drawer, etc.)

 F   C
I need you to help, (can substitute name of a child)

 C   F
I need you to help,

 F   Bb
I need you to help me,

    F   C F
Put this book on the shelf. (truck on the floor, etc.)

 F   C
I like what I see,

 C   F
I like what I see,

 F   Bb
I like what I s-see,

  F   C F
You clean up so well!

Renee Lowry
Canoga Park, CA

TIME TO PUT OUR TOYS AWAY

Sung to: "Here We Go Around the Mulberry Bush"

  D   D   A   A
It's time to put our toys away, toys away, toys away.

  D   D   A   D
It's time to put our toys away so we can eat our lunch.

(You may substitute other phrases for "eat our lunch" such as play outside,
go to music, etc.)

MaryAnn Adams
Manassas, VA

KINDERGARTEN HERE WE COME

Sung to: "Oh My Darling"

       C   C
Oh, we're ready, oh we're ready,

    C   G
To leave preschool

       F   C
We've learned many things

      G   C
And had lots of fun too.

          C   C
So we're ready, so we're ready,

      C   G
Kindergarten, here we come,

      F   C
We are looking so happy,

      G   C
Cause school will be fun.

Valerie Bielsker
Overland Park, KS

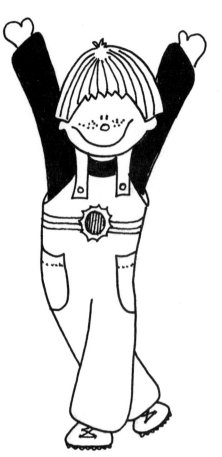

OFF TO KINDERGARTEN

Sung to: "Oscar Meyer Theme Song"

      F   G
Oh, I'm ready to go off to kindergarten

C   F Bb C
That is where I really want to beeeee....

     F   G
Cause when I go off to kindergarten,

C   F
Everyone will think I'm really neeeat.

Valerie Bielsker
Overland Park, KS

NOW THE DAY IS OVER

Sung to: "Mickey Mouse Club Song"

F
Now the day is over

        G   C
It's time to say goodbye.

F   F7   Bb   Bbm
Goodbye to you, go in peace

F   C7   F
Go in God's peace.

Carol Preston
Milpitas, CA

SONGS ABOUT ME

SPECIAL ME

Sung to: "Twinkle, Twinkle Little Star"

```
C          C         F        C
Special, Special, Special Me  (points to self)

F        C      G7      C
How I wonder what I'll be  (hands under chin, wondering)

C         F         C     G7
In this big world I can be  (circle hands resembling earth)

C        F      C      G7
Anything I want to be.

C          C         F        C
Special, Special, Special Me,

F        C      G7      C
How I wonder what I'll be.
```

Kristine Wagoner
Pacific, WA

S - M - I - L - E

Sung to: "Don't Sit Under the Apple Tree"

    C   C   C
It isn't any trouble just to S - M - I - L - E

    G7   C
    S - M - I - L - E, S - M - I - L - E.

    C   C   C
It isn't any trouble just to S - M - I - L - E,

    G7   G7   C
If you only take the trouble just to S - M - I - L - E.

Linda Robinson
Centerville, MA

LOVE

Sung to: "Row, Row, Row Your Boat"

F
Love, love is all around.

F
It will grow with you.

F
Show it, tell it, feel it, share it.

C   F
Make it part of you.

Adele Engelbracht
River Ridge, LA

ARE YOU SMILING?

Sung to: "Frere Jacques"

 C   C
Are you smiling, are you smiling?

  C   C
I like you, I like you!

 C   C
This is such a nice place for a sunny bright face,

  C   C
I like you, I like you!

Mildred Hoffman
Tacoma, WA

TEARS, TEARS, GO AWAY

Sung to: "Rain, Rain, Go Away"

 C
Tears, tears, go away,

Come again some other day.

 G
Tears, tears, go away,

                      C   C
Little (child's name) wants to play.

Sister Linda Kaman R.S.M.
Pittsburgh, PA

66

IF YOU GET LOST

Sung to: "Yankee Doodle"

   F   C
If you get lost on any street

   F   C
Don't talk to any stranger

         F
Look for a policeman and he wi-ll

C   F
Keep you out of danger.

Bb
Tell him what you name is

  F
Where your house is too

Bb
He will help you get back home

  C   F
Or bring your Mom to you!

Judy Hall
Wytheville, VA

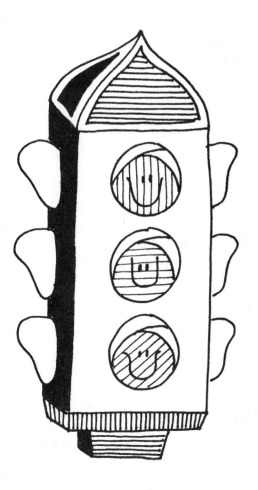

BUCKLE UP

Sung to: "A-Hunting We Will Go"

       F
The wheels go round and round   (Arms move in circular motion)

      F
We drive the car in town   (Drive like we're steering)

   F
We buckle up   (Buckle seat belt)

   F
In case we stop   (Hold out palm)

    F   C   F
So we'll be safe and sound.   (Cuddle ourselves)

Judy Hall
Wytheville, VA

WHEN I CROSS THE STREET

Sung to: "Have You Ever Seen A Lassie?"

     C   C   G   C
Wh-en I cross the street, the street, the street

     C   C   G   C
Wh-en I cross the street, I make sure that I'm safe.

 G   C   G   C
I look this way and that way, and that way and this way,

     C   C   G   C
Wh-en I cross the street, I make sure that I'm safe.

Frank Dally
Akeny, IA

SAFETY

Sung to: "Twinkle, Twinkle Little Star"

C
Red means stop and

F   C
Green means go —

G7   C
Yellow watch out, you

G7   C
Better go slow!

C   F
Keep your eye right

C   G7
On the light —

C   F
It will tell you

C   G7 C
What is right!

Let the children hold different
colors of stoplight and stand up
when color is sung.

Judy Hall
Wytheville, VA

MANNERS

Sung to: "Hickory, Dickory, Dock"

<pre>
  C   G   C
Cover your mouth when you cough,

  C   G   C
Cover your mouth when you sneeze.

C   G   C   G
If you cough or if you sneeze -

  C   G   C
Cover your mouth if you please.
</pre>

Ruth Miller
San Antonio, TX

WASH, WASH, WASH YOUR HANDS

Sung to: "Row, Row, Row Your Boat"

<pre>
F
Wash, wash, wash your hands   (Face can be used too)

F
Wash them day and night

F
Soap and water does the trick

        C   F
It keeps them clean and bright!

F
Brush, brush, brush your teeth

F
Use some toothpaste too!

F
Brush up and down and all around

     C   F
And eat what's right for you!
</pre>

Judy Hall
Wytheville, VA

I BRUSH MY TEETH

Sung to: "Jingle Bells"

G   G
I brush my teeth, I brush my teeth,
G   C   G
Morning, noon, and night.

  C   G
I brush them, floss them, rinse them clean
  A7   D7
I keep them nice and white.

  G   G
I brush them once, I brush them twice,
  G   C   G
I brush them till they shine.
  C   G
I always brush them up and down,
      D7   G
Those precious teeth of mine.

  G   G
I eat good foods, I eat good foods,
  G   C   G
I give my teeth a treat.
  C   G
I always eat fruits, breads, and milk,
A7   D7
Vegetables and meat.

  G   G
If I eat sweets, if I eat sweets,
  G   C   G
I brush them right away,
      C   G
To keep my teeth shiny bright,
      D7   G
And free from tooth decay.

Stella Waldron
Lincoln, NE

GET MY TOOTHPASTE, GET MY BRUSH

Sung to: "Twinkle, Twinkle Little Star"

C   C   F   C
Get my toothpaste, get my brush.
G7   C   G7   C
I won't hurry, I won't rush.
C   G7   C   G7
Making sure my teeth are clean.
C   G7   C   G7
Front and back and in-between.
C   F   C
When I brush for quite a while,
G7   C   G7   C
I will have a happy smile.

Frank Dally
Akeny, IA

A TOOTHBRUSH

Sung to: "Yankee Doodle"

          C   C
Of all the things around the town
        C   G
A toothbrush is a dandy
          C   C
Brush up and down and all around
        G   C
And stay away from candy.

Florence Dieckmann
Roanoke, VA

69

NAMING THE PARTS OF THE BODY

Sung to: "Twinkle, Twinkle Little Star"

    C   F   C
1. If a bird you want to hear,

        F   C   G7   C
   You have to listen with your _____. (ears)

    C   F   C
2. If you want to dig in sand,

       F   C   G7   C
   Hold the shovel in your _____. (hand)

      C   F   C
3. To see an airplane as it flies,

      F   C   G7   C
   You must open up your _____. (eyes)

      C   F   C
4. To smell a violet or a rose

      F   C   G7   C
   You sniff the fragrance through your _____. (nose)

    C   F   C
5. When you walk across the street,

      F   C   G7   C
   You use two things you call your _____. (feet)

    C   F   C
6. East and West and North and South,

      F   C   G7   C
   To eat or talk you use your _____. (mouth)

Mrs. Gary McNitt
Adrian, MI

ON EACH HAND I HAVE FIVE FINGERS

Sung to: "Old MacDonald Had a Farm"

C   C   F   C
On each hand I have five fingers,

C   G7   C
One, two, three, four, five.

      C
With five fingers here,

C
Five fingers there,

C   C
Each hand has five fingers,

C   F   C
All together now let's count,

C   G   C
One, two, three, four, five.

Saundra Winnett
Fort Worth, TX

FINGER SONG

Sung to: "ABC Song"

C   F   C
1, 2, 3, 4, 5 fingertips,

F   C   G7   C
I can touch them to my lips.

C   F   C   G7
I can cover up my eyes,

C   G7   C   G7
I can clap them on my thighs.

C   F   C
Now let's do the other hand,

F   C   G7   C
Are you sure you understand?

(Repeat)

Mildred Hoffman
Tacoma, WA

SHOW ME IF YOU CAN

Sung to: "In and Out The Window"

F   C
Whe-ere is your finger?

C   F
Whe-ere is your finger?

F   C
Whe-ere is your finger?

C   F
Show me if you can.

F   C
Good, now where's your nose?

C   F
Now, where is your nose?

F   F
Now, where is your nose?

C   F
Show me if you can.

(Continue with other body parts)

Barbara Robinson
Glendale, AZ

THIS IS THE WAY

Sung to: "London Bridge"

C   C
This is the way we feel our muscles,

G   C
Feel our muscles, feel our muscles,

C   C
This is the way we feel our muscles

G   C
Right before we punch. (pretend to punch)

C   C
This is the way we use our lungs,

G   C
Use our lungs, use our lungs,

C   C
This is the way we use our lungs,

G   C
To blow out birthday candles. (blow out candles)

C   C
This is the way we feel our heart,

G   C
Feel our heart, feel our heart,

C   C
This is the way we feel our heart

G   C
Beating up and down, thump-thump . . . (feel your heart)

Valerie Bielsker
Overland Park, KS

WAKE UP SLEEPY HEADS

Sung to: "Yankee Doodle"

C   C   G7
Hey, you sleepy heads, wake up

     C   G
You cannot sleep all day.

     C   F
It's time to open up your eyes

     G7   C
So we can run and play.

F
Find your shoes and put them on.

    C
We'll put your cot away.

F
We are rested from our nap

    C   G7   C
And now we want to play.

> Frank Dally
> Ankeny, IA

TOUCH MY NOSE

Sung to: "Twinkle, Twinkle Little Star"

C   C   F   C
Wiggle wiggle little toes

F   C   G7   C
Oh! my goodness what a pose.

C   F   C   G7
Up above my head so high

C   G7   C   G7
Dancing way up in the sky.

C   C   F   C
Wiggle, wiggle little toes

F   C   G7   C
Won't you come and <u>touch</u> my nose.

(With your infant on his back, grasp his ankles and "dance" his feet around in the air. On the last line, bring his feet down to touch the child's nose. My 9 month-old would get so excited he'd grab at his feet half way through the song wanting them to hurry up and "touch the nose.")

> Julie Marr
> Altadena, CA

PEEK A BOO

Sung to: "Frere Jacques"

Where are you hiding?

C
Where are you hiding?

C
I can't see you.

C
I can't see you.

C
Are you here or over there?

C
Are you here or over there?

C   C
Peek a boo!

C   C
Peek a boo!

Cover eyes with your hands at beginning of song and take away at end.

> Pat Cook
> Hartford, VT

SONGS ABOUT ANIMALS

I HEAR THE ANIMALS

Sung to: "Frere Jacques"

F   F
I hear pigs, I hear pigs

F   F
Hear them grunt, hear them grunt

F
Grunt-grunt-grunt-grunt-grunt-grunt

F
Grunt-grunt-grunt-grunt-grunt-grunt

F   F
Hear them grunt, hear them grunt.

F   F
I hear cats, I hear cats

F   F
Hear them meow, hear them meow

F
Meow-meow-meow-meow-meow-meow

F
Meow-meow-meow-meow-meow-meow

F   F
Hear them meow, hear them meow.

(Let children name other animals and the sounds they make.)

Jean Warren

73

CRAWL, CRAWL, LITTLE SNAKE

Sung to: "Twinkle, Twinkle, Little Star"

C   F   C
Crawl, crawl little snake,

G7   C   G7   C
When I see you, how I shake.

C   F   C   G7
Crawling all around the yard,

C   F   C   G7
On your tummy, it's so hard.

C   F   C
Crawl, crawl little snake,

G7   C   G7   C
When I see you how I shake.

C   F   C
Wiggle, wiggle little worm,

G7   C   G7   C
Oh, how you do like to squirm.

C   F   C   G7
Wiggling in the grass and dirt,

C   F   C   G7
Doesn't all that wiggling hurt?

C   F   C
Wiggle, wiggle little worm,

G7   C   G7   C
How I like to see you squirm.

C   F   C
Swim, swim, little fish,

G7   C   G7   C
Oh, how you do like to swish.

C   F   C   G7
Splishing, splashing to and fro.

C   F   C   G7
Sometimes fast and sometimes slow.

C   F   C
Swim, swim little fish,

G7   C   G7   C
How I like to see you swish.

LITTLE TADPOLE

Sung to: "Frere Jacques"

F   F
Little tadpole, Little tadpole

F   F
Lost his tail, lost his tail.

F
Now he has two feet

F
Now he has four feet

F   F
Look a frog! Look a frog!

Linda Warren
Newberry Park, CA

C   F   C
Buzz, buzz little bee,

G7   C   G7   C
Buzzing, buzzing right past me.

C   F   C   G7
Stopping at each flower you meet.

C   F   C   G7
Spreading pollen with your feet.

C   F   C
Buzz, buzz little bee.

G7   C   G   C
Buzz, buzz right past me.

Stella Waldron
Lincoln, NE

BIRDS FLY HIGH

Sung to: "Twinkle, Twinkle Little Star"

C   F C
Birds fly high and bees fly low,

G7   C G7 C
Caterpillars crawl and rivers flow,

C G7 C   G7
Cats meow and cows go "moo."

C G7 C   G7
Puppies bark and babies "coo."

C   F C
So many things to see and hear,

G7 C   G7 C
I use my eyes and I use my ears.

Use as a fingerplay, too.

Barbara Robinson
Glendale, AZ

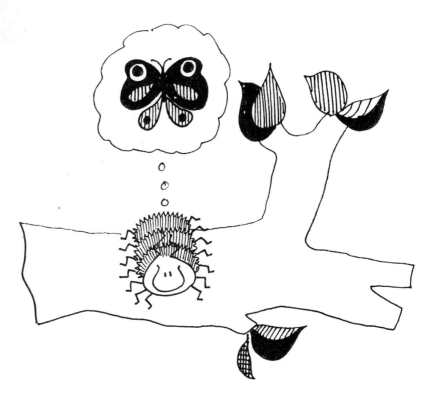

BUGS

Sung to: "Frere Jacques"

F
Big bugs, small bugs,

F
Big bugs, small bugs,

F
See them crawl

F
On the wall?

F
Creepy, creepy, crawly,

F
Never, never falling.

F
Bugs, bugs, bugs,

F
Bugs, bugs, bugs.

Irmgard Fuertges
Kitchner, Ontario

PRETTY BUTTERFLY (METAMORPHOSIS)

Sung to: "Up On The House Top"

F
First comes a butterfly and lays an egg,

Bb   F   C7
Out comes the caterpillar with many legs.

F
Oh, see the caterpillar spin and spin,

 Bb   F   C F
A little cocoon (chrysalis) to sleep in.

Bb   Am   D7
Oh, oh, oh, look and see

Gm C7 F
Oh, oh, oh, look and see

F   Bb F Bdim.
Out of the cocoon (chrysalis) my, oh, my,

F   Gm C7 F
Out comes a pretty butterfly.

Stella Waldron
Lincoln, NE

ALL ABOUT DINOSAURS

Sung to: "Mary Had a Little Lamb"

C   C   G   C
Dinosaurs are very big, very big, very big,

C   C   G   C
Dinosaurs are very big, but most are very dumb.

                   C   C
The Tyrannosaurous was a mean ol' thing,

 G   C
 a mean ol' thing, a mean ol' thing,

                 C   C
The Tyrannosaurous was a mean ol' thing,

G   C
Cause he ate all the others.

           C   C
The Stegosaurous was all bumpy,

     G   C
 was all bumpy, was all bumpy,

          C   C
The Stegosaurous was all bumpy,

   G   C
And he had two brains.

            C   C
The Brachiosaurous lived in the water,

      G   C
 lived in the water, lived in the water.

          C   C
The Brachiosaurous lived in the water,

     G   C
Because he only ate plants.

     C   C
The Trachodon had 2000 teeth,

    G   C
 2000 teeth, 2000 teeth,

     C   C
The Trachodon had 2000 teeth

 G   C
So he was called rough-toothed.

         C   C
The Ankylosaurous's back was curved

          G   C
 back was curved, back was curved,

         C   C
The Ankylosaurous's back was curved,

     G   C
That's how he got his name.

         C   C
The Brontosaurous was very big,

  G   C
 very big very big,

         C   C
The Brontosaurous was very big,

 G   C
And lived with Fred Flintstone.

C   C
Now you know about dinosaurs,

     G   C
 about dinosaurs, about dinosaurs,

C   C
Now I've told you about dinosaurs,

 G   C
So I think that I am through.

Valerie Bielsker
Overland Park, Kansas

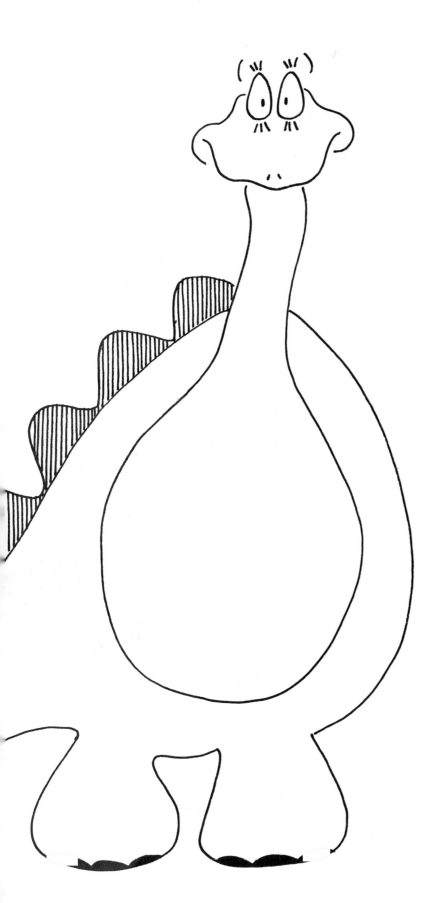

DINOSAUR

Sung to: "Oh, Christmas Tree"

    F
Oh, Dinosaurs

C7 F
Oh, Dinosaurs

       Gm   C F
How big you are to me.

    F
Oh, Dinosaurs

C7   F
Oh, Dinosaurs

          Gm   C   F
What a wonder you are to me.

     F
So heavy,

   Gm
So tall

       C7   F
As you lived long ago.

     F
Oh, Dinosaurs

C7   F
Oh, Dinosaurs

     Gm D Gm C7   F
How wonderful you are to me.

Kristine Wagoner
Pacific, WA

THE FUZZY BEAR

Sung to: "Mary Had a Little Lamb"

C   C
I went to the Zoo and saw,

    G   C
    Zoo and saw, Zoo and saw

C   C
I went to the Zoo and saw,

      G   C
      an animal that looked like you.

C   C
He was small and smart like you,

    G   C
    smart like you, smart like you.

C   C
He was small and smart like you,

      G   C
      but didn't go to school.

C   C
He was a fuzzy, wuzzy bear,

    G
    fuzzy, wuzzy bear,

    C
    fuzzy, wuzzy bear,

C   C
He was a fuzzy, wuzzy bear that

    G   C
    lived at the Zoo.

Carolyn Arey
Salisbury, NC

LOTS OF BEARS ARE HIBERNATING

Sung to: "Mary Had a Little Lamb"

 C   C
Lots of bears are hibernating,

 G   C
Hibernating, hibernating,

 C   C
Lots of bears are hibernating,

 G   C
Sleeping in their dens.

Joyce Marshall
Whitby, Ontario
Canada

BEARS ARE SLEEPING

Sung to: "Frere Jacques"

 C   C
Bears are sleeping, bears are sleeping,

 C   C
In their dens,   in their dens,

 C   C
Soon it will be spring, soon it will be spring,

 C   C
Wake up bears!   Wake up bears!

Joyce Marshall
Whitby, Ontario
Canada

I KNOW A BEAR

Sung to: "Mary Had a Little Lamb"

C
I know a bear named Winnie the Pooh,

　　G　　　　　C
　　Winnie the Pooh, Winnie the Pooh,

C
I know a bear named Winnie the Pooh,

G　　　　　　　C
Honey makes him fat.

　C　　　　　　　　　C
I know a bear named Paddington,

　　G　　　C
　　Paddington, Paddington,

C　　　　　　　　　　C
I know a bear named Paddington,

　G　　　　　C
He wears a big black hat.

　C　　　　　　　　C
I know a bear named Corduroy,

　　G　　　C
　　Corduroy, Corduroy,

C　　　　　　　　　C
I know a bear named Corduroy,

G　　　　C
Lisa is his friend.

　C　　　　　　　　　C
I know a bear named Yogi Bear,

　　G　　　C
　　Yogi Bear, Yogi Bear,

　C　　　　　　　　C
I know a bear named Yogi Bear,

G　　　　　C
Boo Boo is his friend.

> Joyce Marshall
> Whitby, Ontario
> Canada

TEDDY BEAR SONG

Sung to: "Mary Had a Little Lamb"

　C　　　　　　　　　　C
(Child's name)　　has a teddy bear,

G　　　　　C
Teddy bear, teddy bear

　C　　　　　　　　C
_____has a teddy bear

　G　　　　　　C
It's brown and furry all over.

(Change last line to fit description of
　child's teddy bear.)

Examples: It's black and white all over.

　　　　　It's a great, huge teddy bear.

　　　　　It's a huggy teddy bear.

Have children bring in teddy bears. Sing about
each teddy bear using the last line to describe
some feature of each child's bear.

> Joyce Marshall
> Whitby, Ontario
> Canada

ALL AROUND THE BARNYARD

Sung to: "Pop Goes the Weasel"

C   G   C
All around the barn yard

    C   G   C
The doggy chased the chicken,

     C   G   C
The doggy thought it was all in fun,

  F   G   C   C
Ouch, the chicken bit (pecked) him.

Saundra Winnett
Fort Worth, TX

FARM SOUNDS

Sung to: "The Wheels on the Bus"

     C   G7
The cow in the barn goes moo, moo, moo.

G7   C
Moo, moo, moo. Moo, moo, moo.

     C   G7
The cow in the barn goes moo, moo, moo.

G7   C
All around the farm.

    C   G7
The pig in the pen goes oink, oink, oink . . .

    C   G7
The hens in the coop go cluck, cluck, cluck . . .

     C   G7
The rooster on the fence goes cock-a-doodle doo . . .

     C   G7
The ducks on the pond go quack, quack, quack . . .

     C   G7
The lambs on the hill go baa, baa, baa . . .

     C   G7
The bunnies in the hutch go (silently wiggle nose with finger)

John Saltsman
Wenatchee, WA

FARM ANIMALS

Sung to: "BINGO"

F   Bb   F
Was a farmer had a duck

     F   C7   F
And Daffy was her name - o.

F Bb   C7 F   F Bb
D–A–F–F–Y, D–A–F–F–Y, D–A–F–F–Y

     C7   F
And Daffy was her name - o.

F   Bb   F
Was a farmer had a cow

     F   C7   F
And Daisy was her name - o.

F Bb   C7 F   F Bb
D–A–I–S–Y, D–A–I–S–Y, D–A–I–S–Y

     C7   F
And Daisy was her name - o.

F   Bb   F
Was a farmer had a horse

     F   C7   F
And Honey was her name - o.

F Bb   C7 F   F Bb
H–O–N–E–Y, H–O–N–E–Y, H–O–N–E–Y

     C7   F
And Honey was her name - o.

CONTINUE WITH:

   Pig - named Piggy
   Dog - named Rover
   Cat - named Kitty

Jean Warren

I LIKE BABY ANIMALS

Sung to: "London Bridge is Falling Down"

C   C   G   C
I like baby animals, animals, animals,

C   C   G   C
I like baby animals, can you name a few?

 C   C
Kittens, puppies, chicks and fawns,

 G   C
Chicks and fawns, chicks and fawns,

 C   C
Kittens, puppies, chicks and fawns,

 G   C
Now I'll name some more.

 C   C
Bunnies, ducklings, lambs and cubs,

 G   C
Lambs and cubs, lambs and cubs,

 C   C
Bunnies, ducklings, lambs and cubs,

 G   C C
I like Baby Animals.

(Can be used with flannelboard pieces, or pictures
of animals)

Barbara Robinson
Glendale, AZ

ARE YOU LISTENING TO THE ANIMALS?

Sung to: "Frere Jacques"

C   C
Are you listening? Are you listening?

C   C
To the cow, to the cow,

C   C
Hear the cow calling, hear the cow calling,

C   C
Moo, moo, moo. Moo, moo, moo.

C   C
Are you listening? Are you listening?

C   C
To the duck, to the duck,

C   C
Hear the duck calling, hear the duck calling,

C   C
Quack, quack, quack. Quack, quack, quack.

Other verses:

geese - honk	horse - neigh
pig - oink	donkey - hee, haw
dog - bow, wow, wow	bird - chirp
cat - meow	

Janis Lindgren
El Cajon, CA

CAN YOU GUESS WHAT I AM?

Sung to: "Row, Row, Row Your Boat"

C   C
Bend, bend, bend your elbow,

C   C
Move them up and down.

C   C
Can you guess what I am,

G   C
When I make this sound? (Make a clucking sound)

C   C
Bend, bend bend you knees,

C   C
Jumping up and down.

C   C
Can you guess what I am,

G   C
When I make this sound? (Make a croaking sound)

Child acts out the animal and sound and others guess what he or she is. Can be done with most animals.

Saundra Winnett
Fort Worth, TX

SONGS JUST FOR FUN

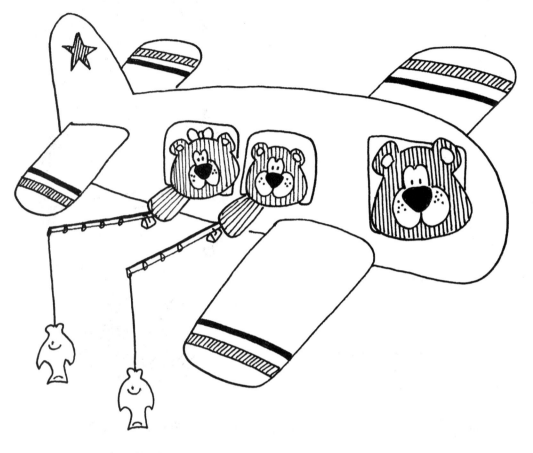

THE SILLY SONG

Sung to: "Skip To My Lou"

      C   C
Oh, you can't take a shower in a parakeet cage

     G7   G7
You can't take a shower in a parakeet cage

     C   C
You can't take a shower in a parakeet cage

  G7   C   C
But you can be happy if you want to.

You can't whistle Dixie with your toes in your mouth . . .

You can't go fishing on an airplane ride . . .

You can't play checkers on a camel's back . . .

You can't ride you bike in a telephone booth . . .

Suzanne Harrington & Wendy Spaide
North Wales, PA

SILLY SONG II

Sung to: "If You're Happy And You Know It"

If the $\overset{G}{\text{sky}}$ is very high, wave $\overset{D}{\text{goodbye}}$,

If the $\overset{D}{\text{sky}}$ is very high, wave $\overset{G}{\text{goodbye}}$,

If the $\overset{C}{\text{sky}}$ is very high

Wink your $\overset{G}{\text{eye}}$ and wave $\overset{G}{\text{goodbye}}$,

If the $\overset{D}{\text{sky}}$ is $\overset{D}{\text{very}}$ high, wave $\overset{G}{\text{goodbye}}$.

If your $\overset{G}{\text{toes}}$ are down below, say $\overset{D}{\text{"Hello"}}$,

If your $\overset{D}{\text{toes}}$ are down below, say $\overset{G}{\text{"Hello"}}$,

If your $\overset{C}{\text{toes}}$ are down below,

Say, $\overset{G}{\text{"Hello,}}$ hello, hello"

If your $\overset{D}{\text{toes}}$ are $\overset{D}{\text{down}}$ below, say $\overset{G}{\text{"Hello"}}$.

If the $\overset{G}{\text{trees}}$ never sneeze, bend your $\overset{D}{\text{knees}}$,

If the $\overset{D}{\text{trees}}$ never sneeze, bend your $\overset{G}{\text{knees}}$,

If the $\overset{C}{\text{trees}}$ never sneeze,

Blow a $\overset{G}{\text{breeze}}$ and bend your $\overset{G}{\text{knees}}$,

If the $\overset{D}{\text{trees}}$ never sneeze, bend your $\overset{G}{\text{knees}}$.

If you $\overset{G}{\text{think}}$ this song is silly, well, it $\overset{D}{\text{is!}}$

If you $\overset{D}{\text{think}}$ this song is silly, well, it $\overset{G}{\text{is!}}$

If you $\overset{C}{\text{think}}$ this song is silly,

Move your $\overset{G}{\text{shoulders}}$ willy-nilly,

If you $\overset{D}{\text{think}}$ this song is silly, well, it $\overset{G}{\text{is!}}$

Mildred Hoffman
Tacoma, WA

CAN YOU CLAP?

Sung to: "Do Your Ears Hang Low?"

Can you $\overset{C}{\text{clap}}$ your hands?

Can you $\overset{C}{\text{clap}}$ them real loud?

Can you $\overset{C}{\text{clap}}$ them in the $\overset{C}{\text{air}}$?

Can you $\overset{G}{\text{clap}}$ them on the ground?

Can you $\overset{C}{\text{clap}}$ them over your head?

Or when you're in your bed?

Can you $\overset{C}{\text{clap}}$ your $\overset{G}{\text{hands}}$ $\overset{C}{\text{}}$?

Sister Linda Kaman R.S.M.
Pittsburg, PA

TOODLY TOO

Sung to: "Looby Loo"

D
Now we dance Toodly Too,

D   A7
Now we dance Toodly Tight

D   D
Now we dance Toodly Too,

A7   D
Lift up your hand on the right.

 D
I lift my right hand up,

 D
I hang my right hand down,

 D
I give my right hand a shake, shake, shake,

    D   A7   D
And then I turn around.

D
Now we dance Toodly Too,

D   A7
Now we dance Toodly Tight,

D
Now we dance Toodly Too,

A7   D
Point to your friend on the right.

  D
Say to your friend, "Hello"

  D
Say to your friend, "Hello"

D   D
Give your friend's hand a shake, shake, shake,

    A7   D
And then let go, let go.

Mildred Hoffman
Tacoma, WA

A FLY IS ON MY NOSE

Sung to: "The Farmer in the Dell"

    C   C
A fly is on my nose

    C   C
A fly is on my nose

C   C
Heigh - o the Derry - o

    C   G   C
A fly is on my nose.

       C   C
My nose is on my face

       C   C
My nose is on my face

C   C
Heigh - o the Derry - o

       C   G   C
My nose is on my face.

       C   C
My face is on my head

       C   C
My face is on my head

C   C
Heigh - o the Derry - o

       C   G   C
My face is on my head.

Let your children continue with this song as
far as they can stretch it out.

Jean Warren

FIVE BOTTLES OF MILK ON THE WALL

Sung to: "99 Bottles of Beer on the Wall"

F   F
Five bottles of milk on the wall,

G   G
Five bottles of milk

C   C
Take one down and pass it around

C   F   F
Four bottles of milk on the wall.

F   F
Four bottles of milk on the wall,

G   G
Four bottles of milk

C   C
Take one down and pass it around

C   F   F
Three bottles of milk on the wall.

(Etc.)

Substitute milk for beer. I usually get the children to shake out their fingers and then we hold up all five fingers and start singing the song.

Besides counting you can also discuss the nutritional value of drinking milk, where it comes from, what other forms milk comes in (ice cream, cheese, butter, yogurt).

Karel Kilimnik
Philadelphia, PA

SOMEBODY'S LAUGHING

Sung to: "Skip to My Lou"

Children may sit in a circle, or stand and move clockwise as in "Farmer In The Dell". One child in center is blindfolded. His is the task of guessing who -- "Who can it be, my darling?"

C   C
Somebody's laughing, Ho, ho, ho!

G7   G7
Somebody's laughing, Ho, ho, ho!

C   C
Somebody's laughing, Ho, ho, ho!

G7   C   C
Who can it be, my darling?

Teacher points to one child who does a solo "Ho, ho, ho!"

C   C
Somebody's crying, Boo hoo hoo.

G7   G7
Somebody's crying, Boo hoo hoo.

C   C
Somebody's crying, Boo hoo hoo.

G7   C   C
Who can it be, my darling?

Somebody's saying, "Can't guess me" . . . Etc.

Mildred Hoffman
Tacoma, WA

SECRET SONG

Sung to: "Frere Jacques"

F
I've a secret,

F
I've a secret,

F   F
You don't know, You don't know.

F
Haven't told my mother,

F
Haven't told my brother,

F
I'll tell you.

F
I'll tell you.

F
Told a secret,

F
Told a secret,

F
You didn't know,

F
You didn't know.

F
Didn't tell my mother,

F
Didn't tell by brother,

F
I told you,

F
I told you.

F
Who knows a secret?

F
Who knows a secret?

F
Do you know?

F
Do you know?

F
Haven't told your mother,

F
Haven't told your brother,

F
Who will tell?

F
Who will tell?

Mildred Hoffman
Tacoma, WA

RAINBOW SONG

Sung to: "Did You Ever See A Lassie?"

       F   F   C   F
Did you ever hear a rainbow, a rainbow, a rainbow,

       F   F   C   F
Did you ever hear a rainbow forget to say please?

       F   F   C   F
Did you ever hear a rainbow, a rainbow, a rainbow,

       F   F   C   F
Did you ever hear a rainbow say, "Icky old peas?"

       F   F   C   F
Did you ever hear a rainbow, a rainbow, a rainbow,

       F   F   C   F
Did you ever hear a rainbow say "Chuck broke the chalk?"

       F   F   C   F
Did you ever hear a rainbow, a rainbow, a rainbow,

      F   C   F
No, I never heard a rainbow, 'cause rainbows can't talk!

(The words underlined may be spoken, not sung, in the most dramatic, righteously indignant voice, which adds to the surprise element of this song.)

Mildred Hoffman
Tacoma, WA

87

HOUSE SOUNDS

Sung to: "Wheels on the Bus"

The kitty in the kitchen goes meow, meow, meow.
C   G7

Meow, meow, meow. Meow, meow, meow.
G7   C

The kitty in the kitchen goes meow, meow, meow.
C   G7

All around the house.
G7   C

The water in the shower goes swoosh, swoosh, swoosh . . .
C   G7

The coffee in the pot goes perk, perk, perk . . .
C   G7

The bacon in the pan goes sizzle, sizzle, sizzle . . .
C   G7

The dishes in the sink go clink, clink, clink . . .
C   G7

The vacuum cleaner goes vroom, vroom, vroom . . .
C   G7

The washing machine goes glub, glub, glub . . .
C   G7

The clock on the wall goes tick, tick, tick . . .
C   G7

The children in their beds go night, night, night . . .
C   G7

John Saltsman
Wenatchee, WA

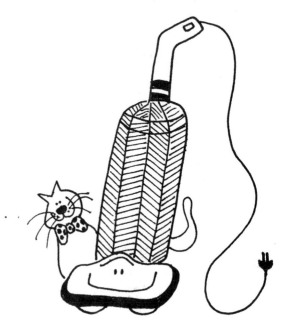

I HEAR PEOPLE

Sung to: "Frere Jacques"

I hear Mother, I hear Mother
F   F

Hear her shout, hear her shout
F   F

Clean up your mess
F

Clean up your mess
F

Hear her shout, hear her shout.
F

I hear Father, I hear Father
F   F

Hear him shout, hear him shout
F   F

Time to go to bed now
F

Time to go to bed now
F

Hear him shout, hear him shout.
F

(Let children change characters and what they might shout.
Examples: teacher (or Miss Jones), baby, etc. Or you could
even go into community helpers like doctor, mailman,
policeman, etc.)

Jean Warren

cques"

bells

them ring.

them ring.

drums

them beat

r them beat.

horns

F
Hear them blow, hear them blow

F
Beep-e-beep-e-beep-beep

F
Beep-e-beep-e-beep-beep

F
Hear them blow, hear them blow.

OTHER VERSES:
I hear sirens, hear them roar
I hear phones, hear them ring
I hear whistles, hear them blow
I hear motors, hear them rev

Jean Warren

CHOO CHOO TRAIN

Sung to: "Frere Jacques"

C
I'm an engine

C
I'm an engine.

C
Need a car,

C
Need a car.

C
Back and hook together,

C
Here we go.

C   **C**
CHOO   CHOO   CHOO!

C
Start out slow,

C
Start out slow.

C
Here we go,

C
Here we go.

C
See me go faster,

C
See me go faster.

C   **C**
CHOO   CHOO   CHOO!

One child is the engine - backs up and
hooks to another child to make a train
and Choo Choo around the room.

Aletha Ballengee
Fort Worth, TX

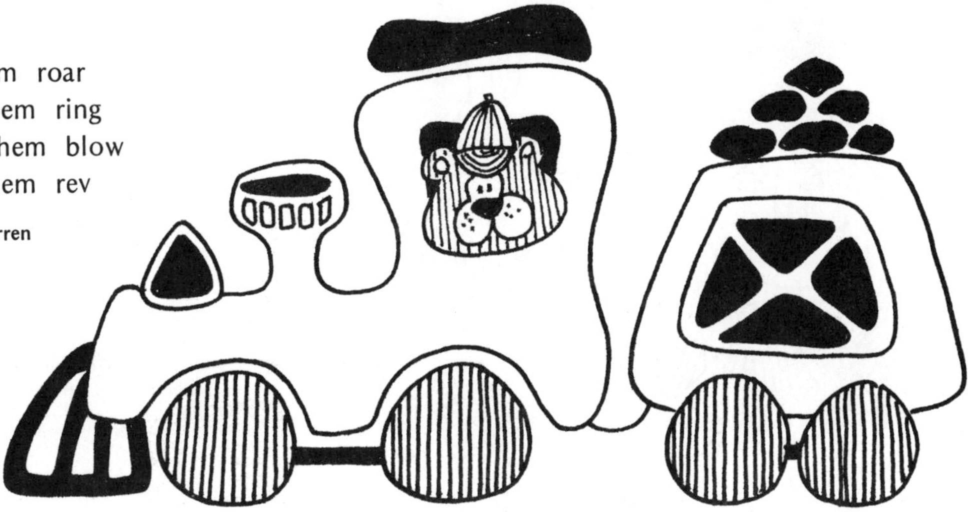

89

THE ROBOT SONG

Sung to: "Wheels on the Bus"

    F   F
The arms of the robot go up and down,

   C   F
up and down, up and down

   F   F
The arms of the robot go up and down

C   F
All around the room.

VERSES:

   F   F
The legs of the robot go back and forth.

   F   F
The head of the robot goes side to side.

   F   F
The buttons on the robot go blink, blink, blink.

   F   F
The sound of the robot goes beep, beep, beep.

   F   F
The voice of the robot says "Does not compute."

Motions may be acted out by the children.

Serena K. Butch
Schenectady, NY

OLD VOLCANO

Sung to: "Frere Jacques"

Old volcano, old volcano,

Is asleep, is asleep.

Sh, now don't you wake him,

Sh, now don't you wake him,

He's asleep, he's asleep.

Old volcano, old volcano,

Is awake, is awake.

Rumble, rumble, grumble.

Rumble, rumble, grumble,

He's blown his top!

He's blown his top!

(Repeat first verse)

(First verse—Begin in crouched position, singing softly. At end of ve
clap hands loudly to awaken volcano.
Second verse—Begin rising slowly-weaving to and fro as you sing.
For last 2 lines—stand erect—clap hands once and stretch arms straig
over head.
Repeat first verse as you slowly return to crouched position.)

Linda Warren
Newbury Park, CA

ELEPHANTS BALANCING

Sung to: "Mary Had A Little Lamb"

C
Elephants, balancing

G   C
Balancing, balancing

C
Elephants, balancing

G   C
On a piece of string (or wooden beam)

C
Elephants, walking slow

G   C
Walking slow, walking slow

C
Elephants, walking slow

G   C
Walking heel to toe.

C
Elephants, march along

G   C
March along, march along

C
Elephants, march along

G   C
As they sing this song.

Jean Warren

MARCHING SONG

Sung to: "Frere Jacques"

C   F
Here we come, here we come

C   F
One by one, one by one

F
Marching down the street,

F
Marching down the street,

F   C
Having fun, having fun

F   F
Now we're here, now we're here

F   F
Give a cheer, give a cheer

F
Watch us dance and sing

F
Watch us dance and sing

F   F
Having fun, having fun.

F   F
Here we go, here we go

F   F
In a row, in a row

F
Marching down the street,

F
Marching down the street,

F   F
Having fun, having fun.

Jean Warren

POPCORN

Sung to: "Frere Jacques"

C
I am popcorn,

C
I am popcorn.

C
In the pan,

C
In the pan.

D
Watch me start hopping,

C
Watch me start popping.

C
Here I go

C
POP POP POP!

C
Now I'm ready,

C
Now I'm ready.

C
Puffy and white.

C
Crunchy every bite

C
Here comes the butter,

C
Here comes the salt.

C
Here I go —

C   C
Now I'm gone.

Have the children squat down as in a pan. Put hands over head for lid. Start to hop gradually standing straight and hopping. Ooze for the butter - shake for the salt.

Aletha Ballengee
Fort Worth, TX

MR. OIL

Sung to: "Frere Jacques"

F   F
Mr. Oil, Mr. Oil,

F   F
Pop our corn, pop our corn,

F   F
You can do it, you can do it,

F   F
Pop our corn, pop our corn!

Sister Linda Kaman R.S.M.
Pittsburgh, PA

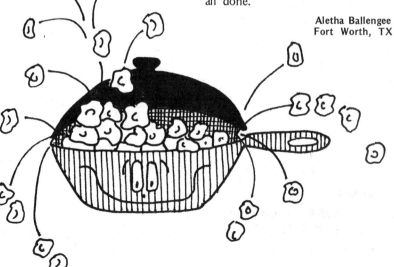

MAKING BREAKFAST

Sung to: "Frere Jacques"

C
I am bacon,

C
I am bacon.

C
In the pan,

C
In the pan.

C
Watch me curl and sizzle,

C
Watch me curl and sizzle.

C
Sizzle, Sizzle, Sizzle,

C
Sizzle, Sizzle, Sizzle.

D
I've got friends,

C
I've got friends.

C
Toast and eggs,

C
Toast and eggs.

C
Put us all together —

C
We are good for you.

C   C
CRUNCH, CRUNCH, CRUNCH.

Have children lay on floor. Start shaking all over as to sizzle. Sizzle and curl until all done.

Aletha Ballengee
Fort Worth, TX

Title Index

Title Index

Title Index

About the "Totline"

The "TOTLINE" is a 24 page bi-monthly newsletter offering creative yet practical idea suggestions for working with preschool children. The newsletter features activities in art, creative movement, coordination, music, learning games, holiday party ideas, science, self-awareness, sugarless snacks, language development plus a special infant-toddler section.

SUBSCRIPTION PRICE: 1 yr. (6 issues) **$12** U.S. — **$15** Canada
SAMPLE ISSUE: $1.00

SONG BOOKS FROM WARREN PUBLISHING HOUSE, INC.

PIGGYBACK SONGS — 110 new songs, sung to the tune of childhood favorites. 64pp. $4.95

MORE PIGGYBACK SONGS — 195 more new songs, sung to the tune of childhood favorites. 96 pp. $6.95

PIGGYBACK SONGS FOR INFANTS & TODDLERS — 140 new songs for infants and toddlers. 80pp. $6.95

OTHER BOOKS BY JEAN WARREN

SUPER SNACKS — 120 seasonal sugarless snack recipes $3.95

CELEBRATING CHILDHOOD — an inspirational collection of poems for parents and teachers. 24pp. $1.50

1.2.3 ART — 200 open-ended art activities for young children 160pp. $12.95

"CUT & TELL" — Scissor Stories for FALL, WINTER & SPRING. 3 books in all — **$5.95** each $17.85

PLAY & LEARN SERIES — material taken from back issues of the Totline newsletter. 6 books in all. (Each) **$6.95**

CRAFTS   MOVEMENT TIME
LEARNING GAMES   STORY TIME
LANGUAGE GAMES   SCIENCE TIME

* * * * * * *Write for our free catalog* * * * * *

WARREN PUBLISHING HOUSE, INC., P.O. Box 2255, Everett, WA 98203

ALL PAYMENTS IN U.S. FUNDS PLEASE